Linear Thinking

by
Maria L. Marquez

Bloomington, IN  Milton Keynes, UK

AuthorHouse™
1663 Liberty Drive, Suite 200
Bloomington, IN 47403
www.authorhouse.com
Phone: 1-800-839-8640

AuthorHouse™ UK Ltd.
500 Avebury Boulevard
Central Milton Keynes, MK9 2BE
www.authorhouse.co.uk
Phone: 08001974150

First published by AuthorHouse 4/3/2007

ISBN: 978-1-4259-8768-8 (sc)

*Printed in the United States of America
Bloomington, Indiana*

This book is printed on acid-free paper.

Introduction

I was misunderstood. Teacher's answers never make sense to my questions at school. My interest in understanding my teachers at school initiated my study for twelve years. I am still learning and believe that teaching is a job to earn the living and that has nothing to do with understanding the students, but with the delivery of the known.

I registered at a private university in Boston Massachusetts and left school before completing my Bachelor Degree and study at home. My teachers had provided me with several fields for me to study and were like converting tripe into a heart.

My effort in learning brought me into the right course and realize that the best way of learning to write is by reading and getting an idea that can be described in own words. Learning the grammar of the English language and meaning of words is very important. The language is our system of communication, and the meaning of words is processed by the brain.

English is my second language. I learned to read and write English by correspondence and registered in the Hemphill's Schools in England. I noticed that the English I had learned differs from the American English used in American schools. The difference created another field for me to study. My intention was learning to write books.

I became fascinated by reading Douglass' Manuscript and the way he learned to read and write English. As we all know, learning to read and write English was against the law, and writing differs from describing a thought. I believe that learning to read and write is the responsibility of every adult; it takes interest and dedication. I discovered Linear thinking and concluded that it is a common way of thinking among all of us.

Faculties

Linear thinking has six common components.

- Focusing deceives, and the teacher thinks as teacher and mixes teaching responsibilities with the responsibilities of the students in the syllabus for the course; authors and their literary works are assigned by page number; an author *not read* is not listed in the syllabus; students are acknowledged that his work appears in the text suggested for the course.

- Assuming allows the teacher to construct words not listed in the dictionary of the English language; words don't represent its meaning and play different roles and syntax is violated; nouns are replaced by adjective and vice-verse.

- The belief in being a teacher allows the teacher to function in the classroom; intellectual faculties are ignored for the purpose of being; job responsibility is violated, and the teacher construct a paper, graded the paper "C", and the grade is reported to the Registrar Office. The New Israelites become the colonists of the colonies; God's plan includes working directly with the hands; struggles of colonists are recorded in a journal for their children to have a history; Separatists is focused as religious faith.

- Perceiving allows the teacher to use the name Separatist to construct the exam, but the term is rooted on being separated from the Church of England in an act of treason.

- Pursuing allows the teacher to construct the syllabus ahead of time; an argument is constructed to define the course, the code of the course is used to function subject of the statement; auxiliary (Will) is used to construct the future as syllabus are constructed ahead of time before start the teaching; the word (docked) is used to define a penalty for late papers.

- Persuading allows the teacher instructing to explore theme or issue seen repeated in more than one author read; the teacher instructs to examine a theme, an idea or an issue in the works of an author not read; the topic on the author must be turned into the teacher three weeks after classes had started, and the author is scheduled for the tenth week of the schedule, and the time restriction is called *timely fashion.*

An argument is constructed to define a course on American literature; the word writing represent the subject of the statement; the argument is constructed with third person singular and present indicative of be and represent state of being of the subject; *critically important* follows the auxiliary of be and complement the subject.

An expression is constructed with auxiliary (will) to indicate futurity as the syllabus is constructed ahead of time before start teaching; the auxiliary function adjective and define the verb; plural pronoun (we) function subject of the sentence and refer teacher and students.

Students are instructed to explore *theme or issue* seen in more than one author read and listed in the syllabus; *idea or issue* refers *an author not read* and no listed in the syllabus; students are acknowledged that the work appears in the text suggested for the course on America literature.

Religious and geographical themes define the themes of the course; geographical refer to the south part of the United States of America where the so called Puritan were settled, but they didn't write a thing; they were member of the Protestant group in the 16th and 17th centuries who had protested against the prelacy of the Church of England; then, they immigrated into America and fabricated the slavery law; the Puritan were self called religious believers who built churches and school and were ministers, teachers, masters and slaveholders and is what is left for learning; the word Puritan is used as an adjective to define *beginning* and refer the beginning of the course; Transcendentalists is used to refer the end of the portion of American literature to be covered in eleven weeks of teaching.

Those themes serve as a backbone for *all American literature*, and (all) stand entire; *the roots of the American Dream* has been portrayed in different ways throughout American literary history, and the American expression is enclosed within double quotation marks to indicate that was borrowed to construct the syllabus, but lack meaning in American literature; the expression was invented in 1933 to refer American social ideal that stresses egalitarianism, especially on material prosperity and beliefs regarding society privileges, law makers and the making of law, and the removal of inequalities in time of slavery was advocated; many American people living the time of slavery were treated with differences compared with others American citizens.

Teacher and student responsibilities are mixed in the same paragraph; grade calculation is the responsibility of the teacher; participation in class discussion is the student responsibility; *Late papers* pass due date posted in the syllabus; papers are accepted one week later after the due date, but *docked one full letter grade*; the word *docked* represent the past tense form of duck and plunge under lower grade; letters are used to grade student's papers; (A) represent the higher mark, and (F) represent failure of the course; *reading in each class* represent the style of teaching, and the teacher read the assignments during one hour class; *Poor attendance and habitual tardiness* are constructed for the syllabus, but are not the teacher's expectations; the word *principle* replace principal; the noun function adjective and define the goal as acquisition of knowledge in American literature; *the paper should be five or ten double spaced pages long and not longer!* While clear and effective writing is required in the process of learning.

A strong essay begins with a strong thesis; the thesis statement is formulated before start writing, and knowing the material is required; *the whole paper exists to prove thesis statement true and applicable* to the work being examined by each student who examine *book of literary* rather than literary book; the kind of sources to write a paper on American literature is defined by four adjectives (historical, psychological, sociological, critical), and adjective indicate kind or quality of the noun; thoughtfully and carefully define the way the papers must be written, and the adverb complement the act of writing.

Early American literature is copied from the introduction of the text suggested for the course; the heading is used in the schedule section of the syllabus; *(see pages l-9)* indicates where the heading was found and acknowledge how the teaching is played; the name of

Bradford is side by side with Bradstreet in the schedule section of the syllabus and seems that the farmer is comparable with the poet, at least, their names begins with same prefix; a unique perspective in the colony's history define Bradford in the exam sheet; he must be discussed as governor of Plymouth plantation rather than Governor of Plymouth.

(Plymouth plantation) was taken from the introduction of the anthology to construct the exam sheet; the experiment of the Puritan is a heading on page (l) of the <u>Norton Anthology of American Literature</u>, Third Edition Shorter, and Bradford is found on pages (32-46) of the anthology.

A paragraph is copied from the anthology to construct part I of the examination sheet "May and ought not the children of these fathers rightly say our fathers were Englishmen which came over this great ocean and were ready to perish in this wilderness; but they cried unto the Lord, and He heard their voice and looked on their adversity" Bradford was English by nationality and Jewish by religion, but he is against the Englishmen; he gather with many others and immigrated into the colonies of England; he settled in Plymouth, Massachusetts and gather with others of same religion to interpret the English Reformation (1550-1607) and built a church in Plymouth where he owned a farm. Separatists Interpretation of the Reformation in England correspond heading of the text; (Book I, Chapter I) is taken from <u>Of Plymouth Plantation</u>, and a foot note at the bottom of page 34 states that the text was previously edited by Samuel Eliot Morrison (New York, 1953)

The name *Decrevecouer* is listed with midterm exam in the schedule section of the syllabus, and he can be found on pages (262-76) of the anthology; his perspectives are colored by political sympathies and immigrant status in the exam sheet, *Report* define his work, and students are instructed to discuss the reason for writing reports.

J. Hector St. John De Crevecoeur define his complete name; *From Letters from an American Farmer* define the heading of the text in the Norton Anthology of American literature; From Letter III. What Is an American on second line of the heading specifies one of the letters written by Decrevecoeur; he wrote twelve letters; *Report* makes the diplomat a reporter rather than author of American literature. "He is an American, who, leaving behind him all his ancient prejudices and manners, receives new ones from the new mode of life he has embraced, the new government he obeys and the new rank he holds" Students are instructed to find where in the anthology the lines were found and discuss the relevance of the lines to the greater work.

Decrevecoeur plays the role of diplomat and indicate that he was also a politician; he views a new land rich and promising, according the French edition dated 1787; he focuses on feelings of enlightened Englishman when they first arrived in the American continent; *the rejoice live to see a fair country discovered* and people feeling and sharing national pride and enjoying their possession, and he refers the land. The author came to the colonies of England as a surveyor of the land and as an Indian Trader and is his responsibilities for playing the role of Diplomat; he was inspired: *The embryos of all the art, science and ingenuity that flourish in Europe* were once wild woody land.

Decrevecoeur contemplates the panorama of uncultivated land in America and imagines the train of pleasing ideas that the spectacle might suggest to the immigrants when first arrived to the land; he brought his letters to London in 1780 and sold them to a bookseller called Thomas Davies; <u>Letters from an American Farmer</u> was published in 1782; the view of so extensive land in a new continent is no comparable with the modern society that Decrevecoeur had seen up to that time; he had seen Europe where *great Lord* possess everything while many others poor people have nothing and own nothing.

Decrevecoeur knows aristocracy in Europe, and no courts, no king, no bishop, no ecclesiastical dominion and no invisible power was known in America.

There were no manufacturers, refineries or luxuries; the rich and the poor maintain a relationship with one another, and that differ from what Decrevecoeur had seen in Europe; *we are people, cultivators, scattered over an immense territory, communicating with each other and united by a mild government,* he states.

Decrevecoeur observed people in a different land and compared the colonies with cities in Europe and their kind of government; he began by playing the role of a diplomat, then, he owned a farm and wrote his observations; there was a feeling of independence as each person worked for himself; remember taxes in modern cities? I believe that the author feels relaxed in his mind; he came to America with a job position and ended up owning a farm; there was no restriction regarding the law; "American Asylum" is called to the land; poor people came from Europe by means of togetherness, and indulgent laws protect them as they arrive into America; they receive titles; the award makes them owners of the land and all the benefits attached to ownership; the immigrants love their country.

Emerson is listed under (paper due) in the syllabus, and in the examination sheet, students are instructed to consider <u>The American Scholar</u> and find out what theme Emerson's Oration share with Poe's Review of Hawthorne's <u>Twice Told Tale</u>; Emerson comments that a group of youth from Brook Farm came to see him looking for help to reform American society, but wasn't a reading man in the group.

Emerson transcends his limitations; he uses his intellectual faculties; intelligence learns and gathers knowledge; the ability to reason concerns our humanity; the only intelligence is consciousness and a thought in the mind describing reasoning; "I am a poet of a low class" Emerson states; he gave lectures in Boston and did tours lecturing in the Northeast; his work <u>Nature</u> is recognized as a major document in American Romanticism and Transcendentalism; "Nature is but an image or imitation of Wisdom"; Wisdom is wise and accumulates knowledge; "the last thing of the soul" hit and discerns inner qualities and its relationship; a wise attitude is a course of action that makes a man wise like Solomon who became the best judge of his time; "Nature being a thing which doth only do, but not know, the true intellectual system of the universe"; the words were found by Emerson inscribed as a guiding principle by the Roman philosopher Plotinos who might exist (205-270?)

"When we speak of Nature" Emerson says, "We distinguish the poetical sense in the mind", "the tree of the poet" is distinguished from the stick of timber of the wood-cutter; the poet is inspired; inspiration is a divine influence communicating sacred revelations as a mechanism of our humanity; and the poet integrate all the parts into one property in the horizon; a thought exist in the mind and is identified by the idea; the transcendent entity is a real pattern of existence and a concept in the mind that comprehends the unknown.

Thoreau is followed by page numbers in the syllabus for the course on American literature; his complete name is Henry David Thoreau; <u>Resistance to Civil Government</u> define his work in the <u>Norton Anthology of American Literature</u>; the intention of governing have complicated the machinery and have nothing to do with keeping the country free or educating its people who inherit what has been accomplished.

Trade and commerce never manage obstacles; *the law of man is continually in the way,* and man is judged by his actions while his intentions needed to be closed; *every person in American society should make known what kind of education is desired and would be one step forward*; practical reason is the power, at least once in the hand of people.

Only the majority of people is permitted and continues for long period of time; the ruling is neither right nor does it seems fair to the minority; the stronger is identified by being strong ruler in all circumstances, but is not based on justice or understanding.

The majority don't decide right or wrong; neither conscience; cultivation of respect for man law is not desirable; man has an obligation to do right things all the time; corporations alone lack conscience; a corporation of conscious men is a corporation with a conscience;

institutions are common result of undue respect and against common sense and conscience.

Marching to obey man law produces palpitation of the heart and is a mere shadow for the reminiscence of humanity; men serve the *State* as machines with their bodies; they stand as an army ; there is no free exercise of judgment or moral sense, but putting on a level of wood, earth and stone; the wooden man becomes manufacturer to serve the purpose of commanding; others like professionals serve the *State* with Linear thinking without moral distinction; others serve the *State* with their consciences; a wise man is only useful as man.

Douglass' Narrative is defined "An author not read", and students are made aware that his work appears in the text for the course; neither Douglass' name nor his Narrative were listed in the syllabus; his name replaced Poe on the 10th week of the schedule; students writing on Douglass' Narrative must turn their drafts to the teacher on the third week of teaching, and the time restriction is called *timely fashion*.

Paragraphs are copied from the text to construct the exam sheet: "Now said he, if you teach that Nigger how to read, there would be no keeping him…He would at once become unmanageable and of no value to his master" Douglass had quoted the words of his master to support his Narrative; the words were pronounced by Douglass's masters when talking to his wife; Douglass expresses that the words of his master sank deep into his heart, stirred up sentiments within that lay slumbering, and called into existence a new train of thought; students are instructed to identify the author and guess where the teacher found the paragraph.

According to the instructions, Douglass plays the role of religion and uses religious discourse in his Narrative, his purpose of writing is believed to be to convince the North part of United States of America of how the Bible was being practiced in the South by the so called religious believers; *Religious discourse* are called to Douglass' quotations of his master words: *"He that knoweth his master's will, and doeth it not, shall be beaten with many stripes"*

According foot note at the bottom of the page 844 of the <u>Norton Anthology of</u> <u>American Literature, Third Edition Shorter</u>, the quotation follows (Luke 12:47); The words were pronounced by Douglass' master at the same time that he tied a young woman and whip her with a cowskin upon her naked shoulders; "God cursed Ham, and therefore American slavery is right" on page 835 of the anthology is part of Douglass' argument on a multitude of people who sprang in the South part of the United States of America and who were born in America and held slave.

Douglass observed that the population of a different kind of people born in America could eventually do away the force of the law; a law was constructed by the so called religious believers to bring people from Africa into the United States of America, but the law was violated by the lawmakers themselves who raped African women and brought thousands of children into this world.

They were children of white masters and African women including Douglass himself, so Douglass informs his knowledge to the audience; a foot note at the bottom of the page state that Douglass' argument is based on Genesis 9.20-27 in which Noah curses his son Ham and condemns him to bondage, but foot note are not part of Douglass' argument.

American slavery is only right in the eyes of the lawmakers who constructed the law with intention to use human being as commodity for the American market, but lack consciousness; violation of the law lead to produce the product right here on American land; the purpose of bringing people from Africa was to have them work for free and build the economy, and according Douglass' explanation, one statesman of the south predicted the downfall of slavery by the inevitable law of population, and there wasn't a need to continue bringing people from Africa.

The idea of learning to write his Narrative was suggested to Douglass while being at the Bailey's shipyard observing the carpenter getting a piece of timber ready for use;

Douglass writes on the timber the name of the part and its intended use; he continues with the italics words in <u>Webster's Spelling Book</u>; then, he learned to read <u>The Columbian Orator</u> where he found a dialogue between a master and his slave; the dialogue resulted in the voluntary emancipation of the slave from his master and obey the master's understanding of his moral responsibility; emancipation is rooted in transfer of ownership and refers to the time of slavery; the slave in the dialogue became free from restrain or any other control from the master.

Teaching slave to read was unsafe and against the law, and according the Narrative giving "a nigger an inch, he'll take an ell" and a nigger should know nothing but obey his master who assumes that teaching slaves to read spoils the best nigger; the suspicion of Douglass having a book was subject to give an account of the time spent alone, away from others, but despite of the law, the mistress and wife of his master had already taught Douglass the alphabet.

Douglass became conscious of the difficulty in learning to read and made a plan to learn without teachers; he made friends with little white boys who he met in the street and convert them into teachers; they helped Douglass at different times and places until Douglass succeeded in learning to read.

Douglass took book with him wherever he went and observed how teaching slaves to read was an unpardonable offense in the Christian country; Douglass uses "Christian" as an adjective to define country; the Christian of the time were so called religious believers; they purchased and transferred African people into their ownership like pieces of property; the Christian had focused on the bible to construct slavery law; they became slave owners, lawmakers and church ministers.

Douglass didn't mind telling the names of the kids who helped him to read, but suspected that they could be embarrassed; Douglass wanted to use the information as a testimony of gratitude and affection for those kids who not only disobeyed the law, but also their parents as well, as it was necessary in order to help a human being desperately desiring to read and write.

Equiano was matched with Wheatley; they both were brought from Africa into America in different occasions; the teacher assumes that Equiano plays the role of religion and used *religious discourse* in his captivity narrative; Equiano was kidnapped, when he was twelve years old while playing with his sister in the back yard of his home.

Two men and a woman trespassed and seized them without a chance to cry, Equiano says; their mouths was stopped and their hands tied up while the robbers ran into the nearest woods with them.

Equiano calls religious believers *Nominal Christians* to mean Christian in name only; the kind of Christian were not practicing according human principles; Equiano believes that they had torn African men and women from their country and friends for the luxury and lust of so called Christians; tender feelings of the African people are sacrificed to satisfy avarice of the Christians; Equiano always found other people who understood him; he observed that the languages of different nations don't differ much; he learned three different languages in the way from Africa; he also encountered misery and suffering for Christian prosperity who mingled with adversity and bitterness; the heaven protect the weak from the strong, he states; the victims falls in the violence of the African trader who help the Christian to get human commodity, and the market doesn't differ from any other market.

Christian relate Christianity; the noun was used in (1526) to explain belief in the teaching of Jesus Christ; the so called religious believers had emigrated into American from England where they protested against the Church of England; they settled in the South under the name Puritan; the construction of the law together with using human beings as commodity is their practice against morality; their belief in being pure convict them and explain their state of being convinced.

"When I looked round the ship, and saw a large furnace of copper boiling and a multitude of black people of every description chained together, every one of their countenances expressing dejection and sorrow, I no longer doubted of my fate; and quite overpowered with horror and anguish I fell motionless on the deck and fainted", but should state felt motionless and fainted; the paragraph was copied to construct part I of final examination, and students are instructed to guess where the teacher found the paragraph and to identify the author and the name of the literary piece; literary works are assigned by page number.

Equiano observed that all the people seem in the way to America resembled in manners, customs and languages except those who doesn't circumcise (not Jewish); the women drink and sleep with their men, and not sacrifices or offering among them was observed; after he recovered from the view of the furnace boiling and the multitude of black people chained together seen in the ship, he saw unchained black people around him and thought that they were paid for his kidnapping; Equiano asked if others man in the ship with red faces and long hair were supposed to eat him; the twelve years old boy didn't know the purpose of his kidnapping.

The boy observed the white male as carnivorous animals who eat meat; the child felt fear and unpleasant emotion at his experience; parents lose their children, brothers their sisters, husband their wives; the trade is a refinement of cruelty, say Equiano with no advantage, but aggravation and distress added to the horror of wretchedness of slavery.

Wheatley belongs with Equiano; her name is followed by page numbers in the schedule section of the syllabus; Phillis Wheatley was only nineteen years old when her poems were published in London in 1773; <u>On Being Brought from Africa to America</u> entitles her poem.

"Mercy brought me from my pagan land
Taught my...soul to understand that there's a
God—that there's a Savior too
Once I redemption neither sought nor knew...
Some view our sable race with scornful eye
Their color is a diabolic dye
Remember, Christians, Negroes, black as Cain,
May be refined, and join the Angelic train

The word *excerpts is used to* define two captivity narratives corresponded to Equiano and Rowlandson; (excerpt) selects for quoting; *Community Utterances* is quoted, and the teacher acknowledge that borrowed Professor Gate's phrase; the teacher states in the exam that the phrase was imitated in the author's respective communities, and according the exam, there are similarities and major differences that corroborate with the quotation; in reality, Equiano is a black man and writes for black people; Rowlandson is a white woman and writes for white people; they are matched under captivity narrative; their work became great literary successes as well as important, and their work are issues of self reliance and reliance on faith, and the exam question asks for *issue* addressing *the dominant cultures of the two authors.*

Irving belongs with Fuller and is followed by correspondent number of pages in the schedule section of the syllabus; Washington Irving existed (1783-1859) and became the first American who achieved international literary reputation; <u>Rip Van Winkle</u> represent name of his tale found among the papers of an old gentleman of New York who was curious about the Dutch history of the Province, in the manners described, and in the descendants from primitive settlers.

The Dutch family of Irving lived in a low roofed farm house; the play was appreciated as a little clasped volume of typeface in early printed books resembling medieval script; such books were equipped with clasps, so the books could be shut and locked; the story of the Province relate the reign of the Dutch governor.

Shapes of the mountain regarded the good wives, for and near as perfect barometers at the food of the mountain; the voyager describes the light smoke curling up from a village; shingle roofs gleam the trees; the blue tints of the upland melt away into fresh green landscape; the village of great antiquity is found in the Dutch colonists; the early time of the Province begins with the good Peter Stuyvesant (Play writer).

The houses of the original settlers stands within a few years with lattice windows; gable fronts surmounted with weather cocks and were built with bricks brought from Holland; the village was settled in a Province of Great Britain; Rip Van Winkle descends from the chivalrous days of Peter Stuyvesant and inherit little character from his ancestors, he was a simple good natured man, a kind neighbor, obedient and a henpecked husband.

Rip's compositions detect insuperable aversion to profitable labor; he never refused to assist neighbors and was used by the woman in the village to run errands, do little odd jobs as their husband don't do for them; Rip was ready to attend anybody business, but his own.

Others copied paragraphs follow as appears in part one of final examination sheet: "The Heaven I desired was a heaven of holiness, to be with God and to spend my eternity in divine love, and Holy Communion with Christ.

"My mind was very much taken up with contemplations on Heaven and the enjoyments there, and living there in perfect holiness, humility and love"

"Whereupon I earnestly entreated the Lord, that He would consider my low estate and show me a token for good, and if it were His blessed will, some sign and hope of some relief. And indeed quickly the Lord answered, in some measure my poor prayers; for as I was going up and down mourning and lamenting my condition, my son came to me, and asked me how I did"

"The mind now thinks; now acts; and each fit reproduces the other. When the artist has exhausted his materials, when the fancy no longer paints, when thoughts are no longer apprehended and books are weariness,--he has always the resource to live"

"During my brother's Confinement, which I resented a good deal, notwithstanding our private differences, I had the Management of the Paper, and I made bold to give our Rulers some Rubs in it, which my brother took very kindly, while others began to consider me in an unfavorable light as a young Genius that had a Turn for Libeling and Satire"

"I am obnoxious to each carping tongue who says my hand a needle better fits"

"I have observed that he was a simple good natured man; he was moreover a kind neighbor and an obedient , henpecked husband--------was one of those happy mortals, of foolish, well oiled dispositions, who would rather starve on a penny than work for a pound"

"Simplify. Simplify. Instead of three meals a day, if it be necessary eat but one; instead of a hundred dishes five; and reduce other things in proportion"

"Were we called upon to designate the class of composition which next to such a poem as we have suggested, should best fulfill the demands of high genius-should offer it the most advantageous field of exertion-we should unhesitatingly speak of the prose tale, as------has here exemplified it. We allude to the short prose narrative, requiring from a half-hour to one or two hours in its perusal"

My mid-term exam was rejected because its content didn't satisfy my teacher expectations; a new paper was constructed by my teacher who graded her paper "C" and reported the grade to the Registrar Office; the low mark indicates that the teacher grades her perception of the student; my teacher should grade high mark to own construction, but wouldn't reflect the expectation of the Spanish speaking student; a high mark would detect the Jewish teacher who believes that Bradford used *biblical examples and quotations* rather than quoting from the bible to underscore parallels seen between the colony's early days and the *biblical story of Exodus* correspondent second book canonical Jewish; the Jewish emigration from Egypt is compared with the emigration of Jewish in the English Reformation.

The new world is seen *philosophically as a cruciber* and as a *gift and opportunity* to practice own *branch of faith* and is wanted to be a model nation for *all the world* rather than the entire world be governed theocratically by

Jewish people; but the word (cruciber) is no listed in the 1985 <u>Webster's Ninth New Collegiate</u> Dictionary of the English language; the new world is left for the working of Separatists religious faith; the name Separatist is derived from being separated from the Church of England in an act of treason, by law; Separatist is used as an adjective to define the kind of faith, and *(Br.)* writes true.

The teacher believes that The New Israelites are the colonists of the colonies, that *their lives and all that happened to them* in England are *emblems of God's plan for them*; the plan includes direct working with the hands; Bradford writes about the colonies in a journal and record struggles of colonists for their children to have a history; *Bradfor's focus on* the fact that the colonists were the New Israelites; Bradford writes about the colonies in a journal to record struggle of colonists for their children; the lives of the New Israelites together with what happened to them in the English Reformation are seen as *emblems, and the* new world is granted for the *Separatists religious* faith; Bradford wanted to control the entire world from Plymouth Plantation which is not his plantation but an experiment of the Puritans.

The *New Israelites* (Jewish people) were persecuted by the Church of England during the English Reformation, and they were granted certificates by the English government to own land in the colonies; they descend from the Hebrew Patriarch Jacob who was native/ inhabitant of the Ancient Northern Kingdom of Israel; the colonies represent what is today the United States of America; Bradford settled in Plymouth Massachusetts and gathered with others of same religion to interpret the English Reformation in (1550-1607); the Separatist interpretation of the Reformation in England correspond heading of the text in the anthology; Bradford became a farmer and governor of Plymouth.

Students are instructed to discuss Bradford as governor of Plymouth plantation; his name is used to construct *Bradford's focus;* the possessive noun indicates that he owns his focus; *God's plan* indicates the plan owned by God; *Separatists* is used as an adjective to define the kind of faith; the American farmer writes stories about the colonies and struggles of colonists rather than American literature and built a church in Plymouth.

On the other hand, Decrevecouer's Letters range up the Eastern Seaboard; he sees the new world as a place of welcome for all, where government rule mildly and where people leave *religious baggage* behind and are grateful to the American god; he never visit Charleston, but wrote about it; he is a religious man who makes his way for himself; he writes about how *the nation embrace and assimilate people to becomes less religiously oriented and more American*; the new world is seen *philosophically as a place* for *homogenized immigrants* who are moved away from their religion; he writes his accounts as letters to be sold abroad and make money; The name of the diplomat is written with small (d), and (*de c*) abbreviate his name.

I was no allowed to quote from the introduction in the open book examination; the section of the text is used by the teacher to construct exams; quoting from the introduction brings disagreement from part of my teacher who states that her question was *not adequately answered*, but the argument is contradictory. The introduction is assigned reading in the schedule section of the syllabus; my teacher claims that elements of biography are focused more than authors writing, but my teacher is deceived. Biographies are scheduled in the syllabus; students must ignore the reading of American literature in order to answer teacher's questions which are based on the teacher learning to play the role.

What is the American Dream? The teacher wants to know the student's writing level, and students must write in the American expression; American defines the nationality of the dream and explains series of images occurring during sleep when we are not conscious; the act of dreaming is represented by the verb in a sentence and fantasies.

There are other dreamers with different kinds of dreams, but my teacher is not aware of the fact and asks on my paper: *If every group has a different dream, what effect must that situation have on society as a whole? What are the different dreams? What do they say about the people who are having the dream?* The teacher believes in having the dream in America; I believe that the American dream is to live as middle class society like my teacher without being able to define the course.

I became disappointed after registering for the course; my intent of going back to school was to learn how to write books. I formerly complained to the Assistant Dean and Director, Liberal Arts Program who initiated an investigation about the definition of the course in the syllabus; the investigation concluded in a meeting with the Director who explained that American Dream is an American expression, but her conclusion contradicts American literature as was offered in the school catalogue.

A letter was sent to my attention after two years investigating The American Dream as American literature; the letter is dated August 29, 1995; the word (Discussion) in the letter refers our conversation in the meeting; the Director thanks for my time to meet with her and explains that the purpose of her letter is *to give record of our conversation and provide experience to each student;* therefore, a more successful record can be obtained from the Director, but the job position regarding my educational experience must be clarified, and "*Students, regardless of background, must be able to speak and write English fluently*"

Enjoying literature and having appreciation for its value and understanding our world are just components of *being English major;* other important components for *being an English major* are listed as observations.

- Misunderstanding of terms is discussed with the teacher in private, after class.

- "American Dream discussion" is a situation.

- Teacher's questions must be answered.

- The topic is intriguing.

- Learning to focus on questions and answers is a skill

- Tangential issues are the student's interest.

- Focusing can be learned.

- Resources available help students with issues.

- The course Reading and Study Skill help study skill.

- Reading Skills for College Study correspond the text for the course.

- <u>Fifty Great American Short Stories</u> can be read.

- Working in class room setting help understand instructor's expectations.

- Participation in the course is an extra open elective.

- Workshops on study skills and a group of video tapes describe techniques to improve note-taking and test-taking skills.

- Construction of syllabus acknowledges requirements.

- The discussion of syllabus with the teacher let to know future grade.

- Difficulties getting paper back from teacher is notified to the Director.

- Faculty's comments on Students papers are read in order to progress.

- Keeping a private journal allows to explore topics that are indirectly related to the issue raised by the student.

- The recording of issues of personal interest are used later as a starting point for own personal essays.

- The matter brought to the attention of the Director is an issue related to personal academic growth and can be discussed with Assistant Director, Office of Academic and Students Affairs who can help to differentiate the matter from the personal issue.

- Knowing the student determination help the student in the study.

My teacher of European literature begins the syllabus with an argument constructed with the third person singular and present indicative of be, and the course's code function subject of the statement; 19th to 20th century define the portion of European literature to be taught in 11weeks period; *literary tradition of realism, naturalism and modernism* define the course and *illuminate works of author;* tradition are words of mouth passed from generation to generation without being written anywhere.

Those works influence Western literature and thinking, and master works are works of world literature; introduction to the course realism and the politics of realism correspond the schedule section of the syllabus; Film Vanya on 42nd Street can be seen *if available;* the word *absurdity* is enclosed within double quotation marks to indicate that was borrowed for the schedule section of the syllabus; *(MB)* refers Madame Bovary; the politics of realism refers Dostoevsky; the power of the word deals with Ahkmatova; first, second and third short paper due define the teacher's style; *take home final distributed* stands for the teacher distribution of final exam for students take home, and *take home final due* stands for the return of final exam on the date posted in the schedule.

In another syllabus for the teaching of European literature, the *evolving ideas about human understanding and quest for knowledge* define the course and lead to a modern world view that focuses on the questions of individual purpose; *introduction to course/Renaissance/ Petrarch* is introducing the Italian Sonnet Francisco Petrarca (1909); he fixed verse form of Italian origin that consisted of fourteen lines; *Renaissance tension* use the proper name to function adjective and define (tension) between *Machiavelli vs. Cervantes; Intro* abbreviate introduction, and *Faust the legend and Faust revisited* is found in the beginning of volume II.

Goethe and the English Romantics require no reading, and a foot note appears at the bottom of second page of the syllabus: *N.B Some of these readings are subject to change if the occasion to substitute film for a class lecture presents itself;* (N.B) stands for Nota Bene and is rooted in Latin.

A third syllabus correspondent to the third course taken with same teacher define the course *topics in literature; the New England Transcendentalists,* and Transcendentalist movement spawned in New England; the spawning of 1830's have wide implications as *an American* seeks its cultural identity amidst the upheavals of an encroaching industrial era and pot-revolutionary European influences.

The act of spawning deposit a spawn in America and explain the eggs of aquatic animals that lay many small eggs and product off spring, and working with spawn play the role of spawner, but is far away from the work of the New England Transcendentalists who flourished (*in and around*) Concord, Massachusetts until 1850's.

Philosophical and religious in nature define the Transcendentalists who produced a variety of literary form and product crucial to understanding the roots of American culture; the product produced by the Transcendentalists movement couldn't be read by those who were seeking cultural identity amidst the upheavals of an encroaching industrial era and post-revolutionary European influences.

The definition of the course include Theodore Parker as primary texts and others whose names are undefined; they serve as *backdrop for those artists who in one way or another are influenced by Parker*, but the deal is with Hawthorne, Whitman, and Henry James.

Understanding and appreciation influence European culture in the literary of the American Transcendentalists of the early 19th century; their synthesis of the old is turned with own philosophical and literary renderings and is suited to the new environment of America which is the focus of attention; *Intro to major European philosophy/ Kantian discourse* require reading Nature and History by Emerson; *From Unitarian to Transcendental: Harvard and beyond* deal with Emerson.

Very aspects of a literature refers Thoreau's <u>Maine Woods and A Week on the Concord;</u> *A peripheral vision* correspond Hawthorne's <u>Blithedale Romance;</u> James on Hawthorne and Emerson refers James's Ralph Waldo Emerson and Nathaniel Hawthorne; *the next generation* requires reading Selections from Whitman, Melville et.al. and *handouts TBA* stands photocopies made by the teacher to be handed to students and is to be advised; Notes from the Underground define the literary work of Dostoevsky in the syllabus, and <u>Notes from Underground</u> define the work in the <u>Norton Anthology World Masterpieces;</u>

What is transcendental? The teacher asks the question on first day class, and students must write a paragraph on the adjective for the teacher identify student's writing level; the act of transcend rise above and goes beyond limitation; transcendentalists are people who transcend;

transcendence explain the quality or state of Being; then, the teacher collects student's paper.

Dostoevsky/the politics of realism in the schedule section of the syllabus define the topic for teaching, and Dostoevsky rejects transcendental ideas and found ugliness in transcending; he starts the tension in an argument and became romantic conscious; he borrows money from boss and friends; there is friction with a prostitute who gets paid but doesn't accept the money because is a very unhappy woman and became sick for days after the passionate encounter.

Notes from Underground focus on common being as playing roles and reality and being unpleasant due to low state of consciousness; unawareness torment to the point of shame; an intelligent man of the nineteenth century must be and is morally obliged to be characterless creature playing personalities; the limited creature convict himself and is unable to master his desires; the low level of consciousness is sufficient to meet every day human needs and doesn't allows to be better than what he is and is considered a disease; only a quarter of the whole amount of consciousness is available to a cultured man; human beings advantage the low state of consciousness and purpose (to be).

My teacher had achieved school education, but is unable to meet the moral responsibilities; the human condition of being the faculty keep the professional ignorant as a result of ignoring the intellect; the professional is slapped in the face in accordance with the law of nature; neither the professional becomes a different person nor my teacher desires to become better; the teaching is the pleasure of assuming; the professional ought going inward to acquire knowledge and turn assuming into a thought; real education result from higher states of consciousness taking place by fundamental laws; there isn't choice in reality.

Film <u>Vanya on 42<u>nd</u> Street</u>, in the schedule section of the syllabus was no available at the time requested by my teacher; *Akhmatova,* <u>Requiem</u> was assigned for reading, and *Akhmatova and the power of the word* define the topic for teaching: She lived her 60's for the revival of poetry during the cold war in Russia; poems are universal and stand for particular event; there wasn't romanticism in the cold war, and poets didn't write poems; the idea of power was not connected with the right idea; poetry is about words manipulation and word games and playing games with words; the Russian government was afraid of Akhmatova, but is only American interpretation of her work, according the teaching; Art touches the masses quickly and is *a big idea in a small package.*

Anna Akhmatova, <u>Requiem</u> defines the heading, and (1935-1940) seems the time of her observation; her work is divided in several sections:

- Instead of a preface deals with the terrible years of the Yezhov terror (1937-38); mass arrests were carried out by the secret police, headed by Nikolai Yezhov "I spent seventeen months in the prison lines of Leningrad" (everyone spoke in whispers there)

- Dedication focuses "grief" Rivers cease to flow, the prison gates hold firm, behind them are the "prisoner's burrows" and mortal woe, we hear the rasp of the hateful key, savaged capital.

- Prologue focuses "the dead" glad to be at rest, Leningrad swung from its prisons, senseless from torment, Regiments of convicts marched, Russia writhed Under bloody boots, and under the tires of the Black Marias (Police cars to carry those arrested)

- Sentence: The stone word fell; memory must be killed and learn to live again.

- Crucifixion: "I am in the grave:

- Epilogue I: "I learned"

- Epilogue II: "I see, I hear, I feel you"

Madame Bovary defines the literary work of Flaubert, and M.B. defines the reading assignment in the schedule section of the syllabus, and Madame Bovary parts 1 & II define the teaching: *Madame Bovary imagines herself as a conformist in her society. However, she proves to be the perfect example of the morality that is driven by passions and orgiastic pleasure;* her conflict is between her belief and her conformity, but when she conforms to her beliefs, she becomes confused of own disappointment; her attempts to find happiness in conventional roles as convent student, Dr's wife and farm daughter all failed; these are the roles that society says are fulfilling if the rules are conformed.

Madame Bovary is the name of the character designed by Flaubert; Madame Bovary at school accompanied by her father defines first focus and institution for learning; she was protected by the archdiocese.

She ate at the nun's table and indicate disassociation from the others students; her music class was associated with songs about little angels with golden wings and indicate fantasies learned at the convent, and when her mother die, she made a picture from the hair of the dead woman and is part of the known; she persuades love and married a doctor; she learns to run her house, keep record of her husband's patients; she tries hard to experience love and recite the verses she knew to her husband; she sings songs, but fails to produce love; she wondered whether a different circumstance could have resulted from marrying a different man and pictures those imaginary circumstances.

Then, she wants to go back to the convent, to live in Paris and to die; she keeps casting over the solitary waste of her life and became depressed, capricious and hard to please; she concluded with poisoning herself with arsenic; she left a letter to her husband explaining "no one is to blame"; after taking the poison, she sat down at her desk and wrote the letter to her husband and sealed it; then went to bed; she drank water and turned to the wall; she feels an icy coldness creeping up from her feet to her heart and became aware that her death just begun and was seized by nausea attacks and convulsions; by eight O'clock the vomiting resumed; she hears the ticking of the clock, the sound of the fire, and her husband breathing standing by her bed.

Hedda Gabler is assigned in the schedule section of the syllabus, and according the teaching, Hedda thwarts her own happiness because she is concerned with mage in middle-class society; she gave up Eilert who she wanted to love because he did not conform to her ideas of middle-class success and winds up married to a dull conformist. then, she flirts with the judge to cultivate a relationship with an important man, but winds up being blackmailed; then, Hedda advises Eilert how to commit suicide so that he can make a good impression as she is concerned with her mage; then, Hedda calculates her own suicide for effect and does to avoid scandal, and the hypocrisy is connected to her mage of how one should behave. <u>Hedda Gabbler</u> is the name of the literary piece of Henrik Ibsen and the main character of the play.

Introduction to course Renaissance, and Renaissance tension define the teaching in the syllabus for a course on European literature; and according the teaching, Renaissance allows freedom of art as *big idea in small package* and is important because some kind of truth is communicated to us; Renaissance shifts man into god image and is a classical idea of man as he focuses on earth; Renaissance has no creation theory and has human qualities in Greek; its religious aspect deals with God and questions of intellectual equivocation incorporated with religious thinking, and both sides are of equal importance and value; there is *a binary connection* like joy and sorrow, day and night, body and mind, and tension between intellectual and ignorant; people use intellectual skills while writers emphasizes in god and human behavior for art, but *equivocation* translates being wrong from Spanish language, and the word *tension* is used to schedule the teaching of the time of Renaissance.

European Renaissance form part of the name of the course; the term Renaissance refers to the transitional movement in Europe between Medieval and Modern times beginning in the 14th century in Italy and lasting into the 17th century; the time is marked by works of literature from the writers of that time.

Literary culture defined literature in the archaic time; literary is adjective defining the quality of culture;

literary works define an occupation in time of science and technology.

Literature deals with intelligence and writing of ideas using the grammar of the language; prefix (-lith) explain the structure of the writing, and *literatus* refers formation of the piece of literature as structure; *literati* is rooted in Latin and explain *intelligentsia*; the Latin word is translated as intelligence into English language, and literate explain a person who is capable of reading and writing.

Machiavelli vs. Cervantes define the teaching in the syllabus for the course on European literature, and according the teaching, Cervantes is held slave by his captors in Algeria for a very good reason: *He repeatedly attempted to escape from prison;* Don Quixote defines name of main character and the name of the literary piece, but Quixote didn't understand literature and become confused; no being able to read didn't change his madness of man; the life of the author is not that important; he lived in the time of the Crusade fighting for the right of Christianity against the Muslim; he lost an arm and was betrayed by Dominicans and Spaniards; he was captured in Algeria and paradox took the blame for the plot.

Don Quixote got into the habit of reading books of chivalry that deal with knight skill and distinguished gentleman; chivalry includes the spirit of medieval knighthood with the qualities of the ideal knight and chivalrous conduct; honor is gained by practicing the learned and requires to fight for what is wanted; vocabulary and behavior is learned to acquire power in reality, but reasoning prove a viewpoint; the honor is gained by demonstrating the use of the mind; by reasoning, one can be more powerful.

Faust the legend and Faust revisited schedule the teaching in the syllabus, and *quest for knowledge* is based on pilgrimage and religion; education becomes important, but Faust was frustrated and felt empty after having so much knowledge; he is dissatisfied and expected some kind of reward and answer about the human condition and buy a deal from the devil and his dead is dilated, but has to accept no knowing every thing, and reason lead him to the quest for knowledge, but became disappointed and wanted to move toward a spiritual world, but it only takes place in his imagination.

Romantic age is part of the name of the course; Voltaire, Rousseau/Romanticism and Goethe and the English romantics is scheduled for the teaching in the syllabus for a course in European literature; there is no sense of art and political English literature of the 1700's; Rousseau considered important to know his thinking and feelings, but nobody knows what's going in artists head, so, *it is a paradox;* <u>Confession</u> was not usual as is today *Look at Oprah!* People confess all kinds of things on television; Rousseau tells who he is for people to judge for themselves, but poetry is not significant in the English language; Rousseau said that we have imagination, and Paramount is the work of Artists imagination and support the art, and America produce things that American people want to produce; there are different levels of art, but for commercial, school is required.

According the teaching, Rousseau examines his memory and explains its meaning; he becomes fascinated by his imagination that flourishes meta-physic stuff and operates under *the paradox* pattern, but he put it in a different way; he says that outdoor you can feels your ecstasy; the idea of romance is no meaningful; it is hard to define what is romanticism; the era of romance is paying attention to the passion; there are romanticism in Cervantes, but Machiavelli is not considered romantic; romantic literature is the idea of the super natural; romantic are all the artists together including feeling, passion and emotions, but passion is no described in the English romantic poets.

Goethe is romantic; he says that in order to communicate with art, one need to feel and has nothing to do with the mind, but with the idea of the individual.

The teacher instructs and explains paradox as theology, mystery, film, philosophy and science and change the course of humanity as never done before, but has no meaning to society; before paradox, my teacher says, it was poems, tales, oral tales toward the upper class, the people who could read; edition in Spanish language added more readers; an example of paradox follows: *If we live for ever means over population and no food, and we would die anyway,* and then, teacher's comment: *what is life good for!* Faust is a paradox and was expected to be satisfied, but at the end of an intellectual road, he feels unsatisfied; the mystery is that he needed to die in order to know the mystery, but people sting and go with the flow and at some point there is a paradox; the teacher draw paradox in the blackboard and consist of a small circle inside a bigger circle; the small circle is labeled (true), and the outside circle is labeled madness and moral.

Nobody knows what's going in an artists heads, so, it is a paradox; *madness is a window in the brain with methods for painting, music, drama associated with language*; it is *like a bazaar putting things disconnected together in a sentence beyond of what we use*; artists are not intellectual; their art come from emotions and inspiration and communicate instantaneously if attention is paid; *hypocrisy of films* and *political debate on television has negative influence on people*, and bad influences are learned; art is important because some kind of true is communicated to us.

The day before the exam, the teacher reviews the teaching and instruct students to think in the word paradox as opposite things as *true and right* and how the authors handle paradox in what they cover; the teacher explains that there is a split opposite side of the coin and that duality and tension is paradox; the teacher instruct students to find a set of duality and get a narrow focus that serves as thesis for the foundation of a particular point without going to deep on paradox, but on the surface only; the day of the exam, the teacher brings a typewritten sheet of paper that she called *Base* for the exam and further explained paradox as human behavior and circumstances that manifest themselves in a form of tension called dual motivation that in someway seem in opposition to each other.

The teacher explains that the innate conflict is impossible to separate without destroying the whole; humans can be noble and ignoble, good and evil, spiritual and material; authors introduce the idea of competing and conflicting drives that create paradox, and if we follows Machiavelli dictum, we say one thing and do the other, and *we should simply behave as badly as necessary to get power, so that in the end, we will have the power to do good, and do bad to achieve good is paradoxical.*

The teacher explains that paradoxical situations are seen in the European literature together with others conflicting truths, and the literature must be discussed within that context without resolving paradox because is no possible, but identify paradox without arguing one side of the conflicting duality against the other side; *noble and ignoble, good and evil, spiritual and material* represent the duality and pair of adjectives defining qualities and the opposite; *dual motivation* is tension in opposition; conflicting drives create paradox, and conflicting truths exist in the literature.

Character names are used by the teacher to construct questions for final exam of a course defined "Man, Reason, & the Imagination: Literature of the Renaissance, Enlightenment, & the romantic Era"; *Quixote's ultimate fate, Pangloss's concise view of the world and Cundegonde's brother* represent possessive noun.

The teacher question about the old woman who has a physical wound, on the Anabaptist Jacque, on the character who bring something back from Eldorado; then, the teacher instructs students to explain the cliché: "He's tilting at windmills or don't tilt at windmills".

Cliché in French literature translate stereotype into English language and was used in 1892 by French writers of literature; stereotype cast by focusing, and the teacher focuses to teach; coordinating conjunction (or) in the cliché indicate option between statement and command; pronoun function subject of the statement and is no known who the person is; the pronoun replaces the name; the command begins with verb; the contraction is constructed of (do + not); don't indicate contradiction, and adverb (not) contradicts the act of the verb.

The teacher instruct to pick one of three essay questions or two of the three and explain the advantage: if two of the questions are chosen to write an essay, the student doesn't need to write in much depth and command as is required if only one essay question is chosen; one essay question count as 50 points and requires a full exploration of the subject; either or both Marlow's and Goethe's concept of Faust can be used to discuss the idea of selling one's soul to the devil in light of Renaissance or Romantic thinking in the first essay question. *What kind of a man is Faust and why is he a likely type or character to flirt with the devil? Why does Mephistopheles believe that Faust can be had?* The teacher had used the Random House Dictionary and found the definition of the word hope (The feeling that what is wanted can be had)

According to the instructions for essay question (2), Rousseau appears as an egomaniac in his own writings, and the teacher asks the following questions: *What is the significance of his egomania? What influence did the Confessions have on the writers that followed? How is it a forerunner of Romanticism? What are some of its subjects and notions related to Romanticism?* First, the teacher construct an opinion with the present tense form of the verb and indicate her presence at the time of playing the role; opinion is a judgment conveying what the teacher has learned; then, the teacher uses the adjective of the judgment to construct the first question; the name of the literary work is used to construct the second question; the name of the author is replaced by the neutral pronoun (it) in the third question, and possessive pronoun (its) replaces possessive pronoun (his) in the fourth question.

The teacher instruct to be sure of organizing thoughts in a coherent way and try to unify the questions into an overall response about Romanticism and Rousseau's role; the teacher indicates that the author is playing role in the time of Renaissance called *romantic thinking. Why does Voltaire finally resolve Candide advising that we should cultivate our own gardens?* Essay question number (3) requires recounting *highlights and character attitudes* of the story; the teacher focuses on (highlights and attitudes) rather than meaning of words used by the author; *the episode at Eldorado and the overall theme* are constructed to complete questions for the exam, but (Eldorado) should be El Dorado

The teacher formulates a thesis to be developed by the student : *Madame Bovary imagines herself as conformist in her own society, however, she proves to be the perfect example of the morality that is driven by passions and orgiastic pleasure;* the teacher quote words from the text to construct the thesis and looks for her focusing in student paper; the teacher instruct to find and organize three examples of Emma's passion and orgiastic pleasure and to explore each example by using quotes without bringing any other aspects of the story into the paper.

Examination of society where Emma wants to live must be left out to discuss the parts showing Emma wildly passionate in her affairs with Rudolph and in the scenes with him in addition to the wild sexuality with Leon; the teacher only admits that Emma should conform; Emma's conflict is her wishes to conform, and wild passion must conclude the paper.

Meanwhile, student must change the topic chosen to please the teacher who grade low mark; the teacher can't find her focusing on student paper and is unable to understand that the responsibility with the job is to correct student papers; I *am sorry, but somehow I just don't get the point,* my teacher writes on my papers; the issue of conformity is not elaborated, my teacher states and question on proving Madame Bovary as getting a bad education in the convent.

According to her notes in my paper, convent student, Dr's wife and farm daughter are conventional roles that society says would be fulfilling if its rules are conformed, but now, my teacher switches her focus of conformity in her thesis; the teacher claims that has to work hard to get my point and advises that writing is the job of informing the reader (teacher) rather than making the reader (teacher) work hard to get the student's meaning; *Say it directly and narrowly!,* my teacher states; then, *Find a quote connected to your point,* she added.

You're getting better, my teacher states, *you've a way to go!* Then, my teacher contradicts: *Do not re-write this paper!* The contradiction is constructed with adverb (not) after the verb and contradict my teacher's doing; she is playing teacher while "correcting" my paper and wants me to add one paragraph saying what is being "hit at" and would get her out the hook; then, my teacher writes remarks: *I note that on your margin notes in pencil, on the old draft, you are much more specific than what you put into this paper* but is unaware of thesis formulation; then, she asks: *Why did you desert your notes?* Again, my teacher is unaware that students must ignore own ideas to develop her thesis, and my teacher grades my paper "C" for her inability to instruct the students to write.

I pointed out three institutions Madame Bovary participated; the daughter of a farmer is changed to *farm daughter*; farmer represents the father and define his doing for living, but my teacher convert farmer into farm to define the kind of daughter; being a daughter running her father house must be compared with the father's expectations of his daughter; *a farm daughter caring for her father* becomes failure, according teacher notes; the convent institutionalized the student who lived and studied in the convent, and *convent students* is defined by convent functioning adjective and indicating the kind of student; Madame Bovary brought her learning into her marriage which became the third institution she participated; Madame Bovary practices what knows, but was rejected by my teacher; *Emma envisions of married life and home* must be compared with the way her neighbors live, and what Emma wants must be compared with what society wants.

Remember the teaching of Hedda Gabbler and mage of middle-class success? And how she give up Eilert because he didn't conform to the idea of middle-class, and how she wind up married with a dull conformist? And how she flirts with the judge to cultivate a relationship with an important man, which wind up being blackmailed? And how Eilert is advised to commit suicide to make good impression in society? And how much she is concerned with the mage? And how she calculate own suicide for effect to avoid scandal? Well, that is what my teacher brought to her class and is what is learned to play the role of teacher.

The hypocrisy of middle class success, as is stated, is connected to the *mage* and behavior in society and should be elaborated to prove each section of the thesis constructed by my teacher.

Cited quotes support the same idea, and the words are enclosed within double quotation marks to indicates that has been borrowed; the thesis constructed by my teacher, however, indicate that the words within quotation marks were borrowed to support her focusing of literature; my quotation to support my idea is labeled "Snippets" by my teacher, but the name calling doesn't appears in the dictionary of the English language; ideas are acquired by reading, and name calling is brought to teach as part of the preparation for teaching;

I know it doesn't seem it-but really this is a big improvement, my teacher states in my paper; neuter pronoun (it) twice in the judgment refers her focusing; dash (-) replace comma (,); demonstrative pronoun (this) refers what is being focused and (improvement lacks meaning in the pattern; the judgment is constructed with the present tense form of the verb indicating the presence of the teacher while playing the role; *This is better structurally* refers my paper; the demonstrative pronoun must be used when showing something; the demonstrative pronoun function subject of the argument constructed with third person singular and present indicative of be; an argument is a statement constructed with the auxiliary of be and represent state of being of demonstrative pronoun (this).

Structurally is an adverb derived from structure and complements the act of the verb according grammar rules, but is used after an adjective; my teacher uses words to function in her constructions, and the usage of words play different roles in the construction; the meaning of words are ignored to construct, and nouns function adjective and vice-verse; the structure of a writing carries the main idea; paragraphs are part of the writing; each paragraph develops one point of the whole idea and usually begins with a sentence; several sentences construct a paragraph and are separated by semicolon punctuation mark (;), and a period (.) concludes paragraph.

My teacher disagreed with my quoting from the mouth piece of Dostoevsky <u>Notes from Underground</u> and explained that the character is not the actual author who can be discussed as the thinker; my teacher notices that the character has no name and commented that readers enter into the character's *fantastical thoughts*, but the capacity of an object to think and have thought lack reasoning, and my paper was rejected; my teacher instructed to discuss the author as the thinker of the mouth piece; the topic in my paper following the teacher's instructions had to be changed from (Consciousness, A Unwanted experience) to *Dostoevsky's character*; *after that*, my teacher states: *I see the point you are trying to make, but it is very wide spread and there are many grammatical problems.*

Teacher's formulation of thesis shows what's in the mind: *Dostoevsky's character in Notes from the Underground has in his consciousness begun to think of himself as transcendent. This view causes him to think of himself as above his contemporaries. Their perception of him causes his distress;* the possessive noun indicates that the author own the character he designed; (begun) replace began; (himself) replace him; (transcendent) replace transcend, and (distress) is quoted to construct the thesis; my teacher instructs not to speculate on Dostoevsky's life; the character created by Dostoevsky must be discussed;

the character is no Dostoevsky, and my teacher instruct to stick to the text of the story without guessing about Dostoevsky.

Focusing deceives the teacher who is unaware of the meaning of the word transcends; instead, my teacher believes that my job as an student is to analyze *the text in front* and supply an example of fictional.

If I write a novel about an affair, it doesn't mean I've one; This man, my teacher states, *is in a state of hyperconsciousness* and instructs to see the word *Hyperconsciousness* in the introduction of the text; my teacher believes that transcending is *alternating between seeing society from above and being obsessed by small details of own life*, but is far away from the fact; a person who transcend goes above and beyond limitation and use intellectual faculties to reason and differ from my teacher who is limited to the teaching she constructs.

The word (mad) is quoted from the mouth piece to make comments on my paper, and people behavior made Dostoevsky's character mad, and according the comments, the character knows how people should be in a transcendent world view and comments that is pointed out in my paper, but my argument needed to be clarify for her understanding; the first thing to do is understand that *the character in Notes is fictional*, and the adjective is copied from the food note at the bottom of the page; the literary work of Dostoevsky is a fiction; the author write from imagination rather than observation, however, the description enclose his experience; my teacher can't understand because she has not had any experience and keep repeating *the character in Note is not the actual author*, but her argument contradict the state of being of Note; the state of being is a human condition.

It is not Dostoevsky himself indicates state of being of neuter pronoun (it); the pronoun function subject; the third person singular and present indicative of (be) represent state of being of the pronoun. *You can refer to him as the thinker indicate* expression constructed with auxiliary (can) functioning adjective; second person singular pronoun function subject. *Don't speculate on Dostoevsky's life* indicates a command sentence beginning with contraction of (Do + not) and function verb and subject in the sentence.

Quote so the reader knows the reference indicates a command sentence beginning with verb. The *voice is not Dostoevsky himself* indicates an argument constructed with the third person singular and present indicative of (be); (the voice) represent the subject, and the auxiliary of (be) represent the state of being of the subject. Quoting from the work of Dostoevsky was previously restricted because the voice of the mouth piece isn't the voice of the author. The student must stick to the text of the story without guessing about Dostoevsky, and the controversy oppose; the job of a student is to analyze text in front, and an example of fictional is under condition: *If I write a novel about an affair, it doesn't mean I've had one;* the phrase begins with conditioner (If) and introduce a contradiction; the contradiction begins with contraction (*doesn't*); (*I've*) represent the contraction of (I+ have.)

My teacher comments on the complexity of the character created by *Dostoevsky.* When what the character says *about reason and desires* is analyzed, *the paper works,* and the student *must* stick to that! And quote; my teacher understand as teacher and think that my choice of writing on the assignment in the syllabus *just proved to be too much* but explanation of being *too much* is restricted and *Its led you to generalize;* the assumption is constructed with the past tense form of the verb; (Its) replaces (it); the possessive pronoun function subject, and (led) represent the activity of possessive pronoun; the words in the teacher's constructions violate the syntax of the English grammar and plays different roles.

The teacher's sentence *I don't understand any of this* is constructed with contraction; the first person singular pronoun (I) function subject of the sentence and represent the teacher; the contraction is constructed with (do + not); the apostrophe replaces the letter (o), and being unable to understand represent the activity of my teacher; the word (understand) signifies being below capacity; the teacher had studied to be the kind of teacher to play the role; demonstrative pronoun (this) should be used at the time of demonstrating something. Many mechanical problems are found in my paper which is graded "D" following my teacher's inability to comprehend...

My teacher brought a list of topics for students to choose and write a paper; I chose *the idea of exploration and colonization,* but the topic supplied by my teacher shouldn't be considered. The topic should be Montaigne; his name was listed in the syllabus for a course defined (Man, Reason & Imagination: Literature of the European Renaissance, Age of Reason, & Romantic Age); the name of the author is believed to be the topic and should come at the beginning of the paper to provide the focus

Montaigne argued against Renaissance and colonization, and the student is responsible for finding the reason for *the idea of exploration and colonization*; *Montaigne and his thoughts or arguments are lost*, and an option between thoughts and arguments is allowed; thoughts is the plural form of a thought, and an argument is part of the speech.

Montaigne observed the tribes in the land named (Antarctic) what is today Brazil; the land was occupied by primitive tribes; their tranquility of life, their sense of unification and warfare, their love for their wife, their happy lives, their health were observed by Montaigne who states that no toothless man or disease in their community were observed; Montaigne observed the people living in the land; the "purity" of those people was never imagined by the writers of the time of Renaissance; dancing every day, fishing and hunting include their daily activities; they were happy people before the discovery of their land.

Renaissance tension Machiavelli vs Cervantes schedule the instruction in the schedule section of the syllabus for a course in European literature; the word Renaissance is used as adjective to define tension. Students are asked to write a paper on the time before the Renaissance. Teacher's questions must be focused by the student. Student's topic must be ignored; the word "reading" is circled by my teacher, and *The Praise of Folly* is underlined, and my teacher asks: *How does Erasmus use Folly to introduce paradox? And where is the reference to the idea of paradox?*

Erasmus adopted the ambiguous mouth piece to express his view of mankind, and the teacher found a good job examining some of the tension and ambiguities of the author's work.

Niccolo Machiavelli believes that anyone who determine to act in all circumstances must learn the proper behavior to maintain power; he says that *there is a difference between the way man live and the way man ought to be,* that *anybody who abandons what ought to be will learn something that will ruin rather than preserve him,* but my teacher interpreted my quotation of Machiavelli: *By living well, man will ruin himself.* Being specific quoting Machiavelli makes strong points that *could be discussed as paradox* and it *would be a help* saying: *this is an example of paradox.*

My teacher instructs to be careful; when writing; it is better being narrow and specific rather than broad and general.

The preparation for teaching had ruined my teacher; her focusing of the literary work of Machiavelli deal with *dictum*, a formal authoritative pronouncement of a proposition or opinion; according the dictum, we say one thing and do the other; the paradox is being prepared and having nothing to teach; the paradox is contrary to expectation; the instruction of literature was not expected by the students; when registering in any course; we, students expect to learn from teachers, but are deceived by the teachings; the inability to comprehend is called *issue;* the word issue explains a matter of dispute and a social problem in the subject of sociology; the teacher is prepared to function and focus on competing and conflicting drives as the creation of paradox, and political debate on television has a negative influence on American society.

The issue is that my teacher is prepared to function and has nothing to do with thinking to comprehend, and according the instruction of European literature, *we should behave as badly as necessary to get power and do good,* and doing bad to achieve good is paradoxical, but is my teacher's opinion of human paradox; my teacher asks: *Where is the reference to the idea of paradox?* My teacher claims that the exam question was specific and didn't deal with trends in Renaissance thinking, but formulation of thesis plays the role of teacher. The thesis statement must be developed by the student; the teacher looks for her focusing in student paper while student's topics are not considered.

The teacher believes in middle-class society and use the viewpoint to construct heading paragraphs to be developed by the student: Eilert does not conform to Hedda idea of middle-class success; Hedda is concerned with mage in middle-class society; Hedda married a dull conformist; conformity is a conflict of Madame Bovary; the conflict is between wishes to conform and disillusionment with the farm life; Madame Bovary conforms to what she believes; she imagines herself as conformist; convent student, Dr.'s wife and farm daughter conform society rules; Emma should conform; she tries to conform but fail.

Some words chosen by the student are misused by the teacher to write notes on student's paper; the word (father) is misused as adjective to define house; father's expectation is misused as possessive noun; the word (priest) is misused adjective to define behavior; fulfilling own desires is misused in a noun clause beginning with (that).

My teacher views sex: Madame Bovary proves to be an example of the morality driven by *orgiastic pleasure*; the student must find (2 or 3) examples of passion and *orgiastic pleasure;* the examples must be explored individually using quotes; showing Emma wildly passionate in her affair with Rudolph and the scenes she has with him must be discussed including wild sexuality with Leon, and the explanation of wild passion must be the conclusion of my paper.

The teacher views crime: Hedda Gabbler advises Eilert to commit suicide and is not concerned about his death; she calculates own suicide for effect and does it.

The teacher views corruption: Dostoevsky's character borrows money from his boss and friends to see prostitute. The woman becomes sick for days after the passionate encounter; the author paid for the service, but the woman didn't accept the money because she is a very unhappy person.

The student is deceived by the teaching of Paradox as theology, mystical, film, philosophy and science; paradox are oppose things like true or right; paradox is duality and tension; paradox is blamed for the plot against Cervantes; there is a paradox at some point, and people sting and go with the flow.   Paradox is introduced into America by European authors. Paradox is created by competing and conflicting drives, and doing bad to achieve good is paradoxical.

Dual motivation are behavior and circumstance; people can be *noble and ignoble, good and evil, spiritual and material*; the innate conflict cannot be separated without destroying the whole; there is *a binary connection* like joy and sorrow, day and night, body and mind and tension between ignorant and intellectual.

The idea of Paramount support art, and America produces what it wants to produce, but for commercial, school is required; the product differ from the product produced by the Transcendentalist Movement; they *produced a variety of literary form and product crucial to understanding.*

Thoreau is the first American writing on the importance of human rights and American tradition which is words of mouth passed from generation to generation without being written anywhere. America is a multicultural society now, but not before. Erasmus is material connected with non-material of the world; he was a theological student. A dictum defines the work of Machiavelli. Communication with art deals with feelings and has nothing to do with the mind, but with the idea of the individual. Akhmatova lived for the survival of poetry. Rousseau appears as *an egomania* in his own writings. Spawning define the arrival of the transcendentalists in New England.

A big idea in a small package defines Art, and it is important because some kind of *true* is communicated to us. Freedom of arts was allowed in time of Renaissance. The flow of art is from imagination to the feelings taking world through the senses and not through intellectuals. Manipulation of words and playing games with words define poetry. Madness is a *window in the brain* with different methods for music and drama, and those are associated with language.

Attention to middle-class defines Realism and naturalism; the sociological chaos begins with industrial revolution causing changes and turning toward nationalism and formulation of the nation through warfare; scientific terms are used by scientists to prove things scientifically; nationalism is created by putting young men through war, but cannot be connected with the right idea of power; the land and the world have to do with political idea; America believe in democracy; modernist are people who come at the end of the century; nobody glorifies nature during modernism; the modernism of 1900 relies on national thinking and discovery of science, and thinkers explain scientifically. Literature is manipulated; the subject is treated as mechanical management in a skillful manner to play the role, especially, to advantage the position; it purpose to make living as middle class society. The meaning of the word (paradox) is manipulated, and adjectives are used instead of nouns; adjectives indicate kind and quality of nouns. The teacher lacks reasoning and neither is able to maintain own argument nor answer student's questions. The teacher responds as teacher in the classroom. The outlining of the course detects the teacher's thinking for the role. The learned for teaching cannot be communicated by the ignorance of the intellect.

Renaissance is a classical idea of man as he focuses on earth. *Religious thinking* twists intellectuality. *A binary connection* indicates that the teacher lives the time of science and technology. *Transcendentalists is used as adjective to define Movement;* their literary works are ignored in an argument; the course's code function subject of the statement defined on first line of first paragraph of the syllabus; the definition of the course clearly indicates what the teacher had learned to play the role; the argument represent an outward sign of the learned. The argument makes no sense in the definition of literature; an argument lead from a premise to a conclusion; a formal argumentation reason and draw conclusion by applying reasoning, but the teacher persuades the student to believe in the lack of knowledge.

The teacher thinks as teacher and is guided by the ego; the teacher assumes and invents the instruction of

European literature to meet job responsibility; the teacher is prepared to function and get paid for the functioning. The state of being is constructed with a form of be. (to be) define the purpose of being and the infinite form of (be); (is) define arguing and represent state of being of the subject; (are) correspond to plural subjects; (was) define the belief and represent the past tense form of be; (were) correspond to plural subject; (been) define the persuasion and represent the past participle form of (be); (being) define the activity of (be) and represent gerund.

The state of being is characterized by low state of consciousness; that means standing below capacity and unaware of the human principles for being better being; the existing state of being is translated from Latin *Status Quo* and is inherited from ancestors.

The Status quo Antes corresponds before birth, when one is energy.

My circumstance at school is part of reality and lacks choices; schools are institutions that institutionalize the mind of students; we ought to convert the state of being into a better being and is our moral responsibility. The creation of a thought had allow me the ability to describe my thought in my second language for the understanding of my English speaking audience and is my moral responsibility; making my audience understand me has become my passion.

Bondage is a fact; we are bound from birth and are limited to a low state of consciousness being commanded by the ego dictating to do; our natural condition of being is limited to five senses; the ego controls the mind, and the mind is controlled to stop the ego commands; bondage is a state of limitation; the confinement lack reasoning and prevent from being better; we are born with a calamity, and worse than that is living unaware of the calamity; we ought to learn about our human conditions, but, we prepare to play and is the way we are organized in reality; we function in society and meet social responsibilities; we follow rules and regulations of our institutions and become skilled of tasks.

Neither making lots of money nor having any money directs to happiness; the common thinking transmit non-information into the mind, and the object is no processed; the brain only processes inner information and the meaning of words; objects are stranger to the mind and initiate correspondent consequences; objects fill the mind with invaluable stuff that doesn't deserve to be remembered because it cause stress.

The low level of consciousness can be moved higher to transcend the common thinking; a higher level allows to meet our human principles for being better; the learning empty the mind from objects and trash, and the mind is filled with valuable information; we continue playing roles and participating in common affairs full of love; living in two worlds is learned to meet social and moral responsibilities.

Learning attaches the mind to accomplish and prepares to break the common being without condition; the learning to function makes no human being wise.

The learning (to be) and (to have) fail to provide any thing; common thinking lacks conscience, and a higher state must be acquired; our human principles are the essence of our humanity.

The mind fluctuate different thinking at different levels that are interpreted according levels of knowledge;

the ego brings feelings to the basic mind. The mind is attracted to the feeling; the natural condition of the mind vary; disturbance in the mind must be controlled in order to achieve; common thinking purpose to play roles, and we learn to control the fluctuation in the mind; mental power is manifested by the control, and once the mind is controlled the old personality and attitude changes.

Assuming is the common thinking and is disconnected from our system of intelligence; mental calmness rises from moral practice of "Mind over matter" to come out of illusion; the power include "Paradox and all possibilities"; the determination is a higher state of consciousness that change the nature of loving objects into total love.

The education meet human principles and guides toward best attitude, and we learn by practicing; learning is rooted on our system of intelligence that allows a higher state of consciousness and awareness; the philosophy of morality deals with knowledge of our humanity and teach us to practice for being better being and is the only way of living happy; the practice help to accomplish the goal without recognition of objects; our moral responsibility is to change our human condition and is gained by the practice.

We are attached to a thinking mind and desires and must be detached to learn better ways and help others to accomplish; perfect law takes us from failure to meet our moral responsibility, and no other teaching is required; we become own teacher with a controlled mind; we ought to live with love and be prepared to love and be liberated from ego demands.

Reasoning is free from fear and escape from fate and attachments and is based on the effort to be better and become the best; the apprehension seizes awareness and anticipate great event to the foreseer; intention changes a common being into a better being with higher state of consciousness; being above standing transcends low states of consciousness; a new identity is acquired for the achievement of success; the personality of the role player depart along with the thinking mind; the way to success open doors by a course of actions, and the same person who once ignored the intellect acquires knowledge and ability to reason; being aware of our moral responsibility is the right way; realization is brought into existence and the truth of our humanity is revealed.

An Introductory Note

The banquet took place in Aghaton's house in 416 B.C. The assumption is constructed with the past tense form of the verb; (the banquet) represent the subject of the sentence; the verb represent the activity of (banquet); (place) represent direct object of the verb; the adverb complement the verb; (in Agathon's house in 416 B.C.) represent object complement; two prepositional phrases function adverb to complement (place); (*B.C*) abbreviate before Christ; *Agathon's house* represent a possessive noun indicating ownership; the noun is constructed with apostrophe plus (s) after the proper/personal name.

The word *Banquet* is rooted in (banca bench, bank); the word was used in the 15th century to define an elaborated, ceremonious meal for numerous people in honor of a person; the subject of a sentence is defined on the left side of the sentence; the predicate of a sentence is defined on the right side of the verb. The act of taking is never performed by the banquet; the auxiliary misrepresent the act of the banquet which never takes anything.

Christ is derived from Latin *Christus* and refers *the Messiah* Jesus as an ideal type of humanity. The truth comes as a Divine manifestation of GOD (Generation, Order and Deliverance) and destroys incarnated errors.

Agathon gave the banquet to his friends on the next evening after he and his chorus had offered their sacrifice of thanksgiving for his victory. Agathon represents the subject; the verb represents the activity of Agathon; (the banquet) represent direct object of giving; (to his friends on the next evening) represent object complement; the two prepositional phrases function adverb to complement the act of the verb.

Agathon and his chorus had offered their sacrifice of Thanksgiving for their victory. (Agathon and his chorus) represent plural subject; the perfect tense form of the verb is constructed with (have) plus the past participle form of the verb for action completed. (Chorus) is rooted on Latin ring dance and is defined a company of singers and dancers in Athenian drama; (sacrifice) is rooted in Latin (sacrificium) and explain offering to deity; the God is rooted on Latin *divus* Greek/Spanish *Dios* and Sanskrit *Deva*. God is defined *the rank and the essential nature.* (Thanksgiving) in the United States of America define a holyday celebrated in the last Thursday of November; the thanksgiving dinner include turkey. (Victory) is rooted in Latin *victorious for* wining and conquering; victory defines over coming an enemy and achieving to success in a struggle against difficulties.

The handsome young tragic poet aged thirty-one had won the prize. The perception is constructed with the perfect tense form of the verb and signify action completed; (poet) represents the subject of the sentence, and the verb represent the activity of the subject; (the prize) function direct object of the verb; the word *prize* explain a gift offered in a competition or in a contest.

His first victory was one of his tragedies and first performed at a dramatic festival in the Theatre of Dionysos located at the foot of the Acropolis at Athens and accommodated 30,000 spectators. The belief is constructed with the past tense form of (be); the auxiliary of be represents the state of being of (victory) and define the predicate. (First victory) represents the subject of the statement. The prefix of the word (statement) means standing. The suffix of the word means (mind)

On page (89) Socrates refers to Agathon's courage in facing such a huge audience. The opinion is constructed with the present tense form of the verb; *Socrates* represent the subject of the sentence; *refers* represents the activity of Socrates. *Agathon appears to have been the first to insert into his tragedies choral Odes unconnected with the plot of the drama. Agathon* represents the subject, and *appears* represent the activity of *Agathon.*

Symposium refers the name of the work of Plato; the name is defined as a formal meeting with specialists who deliver speeches on a topic. The plot of the story of the banquet is composed of seven (7) characters; a plot is a plan that assigns correspondent part to each character; the parts assigned are played by each character; each character is assigned a name; the characters represent human beings.

Socrates is fifty three years old, and going by the age, you can tell that the character represents a mature man with experiences.

Phaidros is the name of the character and was invited to preside the meeting*; Phaedrus* is the name of the dialogue assigned to *Phaidros*; the dialogue in the subject of love became famous.

Pausanias is a disciple of *Prodicos* and receives instructions from his teacher who is a Sophist; the wise man instructs rhetoric and philosophy.

Aristophanes is a poet of thirty two years old, and going by his age, you can tell that he has less experience than the fifty two years old. He is a performer of his comedy named <u>The Cloud</u>, and he had made fun of *Socrates.*

Alcibiades is thirty-five years old and is comparable with the thirty two years old; he is believed as a man of remarkable beauty and talent and an eminent statesman, in addition of being unscrupulous and dissolute. His speech at the banquet showed great admiration for Socrates who is fifty three years old and saved the life of the statesman in a battle. *Beauty and talent* is contradicted by being *unscrupulous;* the word define without scrupulous and lacking moral integrity; the statesman represents the standing and is defined by its prefix; the plural form of (state) indicate more than one state; (state) represents the condition of being and the state of mind; the condition is a stage; the word (state) is rooted in Latin (*Status)* and refers the standing. The statesman is the name of the position played by the character who exercises political leadership.

Aristodemos attended the banquet with *Socrates*; then, Aristodemos tells about the banquet.

Apollodoros re-told the story of the banquet to a friend; they both were walking together. The story was re-told fifteen years later. *Apollodoros* represents power; the character was present weeping at Socrates' death.

Apollodoros never attended the banquet; he heard the story from Aristodemos and re-told the story to a friend while they were walking together. Never attended is no being present at the banquet; re-telling tells the perception; the word (tell) is rooted on tale to signify relate or narrate. Hearing has capacity of perceiving the words spoken by someone else, but the perception gain no-information and nothing is learned. The word attempt, on the other hand, is rooted on (touch), and Apollodoros was weeping at Socrates' death; the weeper expresses deep sorrow by the shedding of tears.

The Story of the Banquet According Apollodoros

Apollodoros believes in being *pretty well word-perfect)*; he was approaching to town, and someone he knew caught sight of him. Catching seizes and capture after pursuing the sight; the definition of the word catching is assumed in the 1985 Webster's Ninth New Collegiate dictionary. Apollodoros was called from behind, some distance away, in a bantering tone; calling is rooted in (voice) and (talking loud); the word calling is defined as speaking in a loud, distant voice, so as to be heard at a distance. The voice shouted: *Apollodoros Halt*; shouting utter a loud cry commanding attention to stop, and Apollodoros obeyed the command and stop and *stood still*.

Apollodoros heard the voice saying: *Well, Apollodoros, I was just looking for you.* The heard by Apollodoros knows about the banquet at Agathon's party. Socrates, Alcibiades and others were present at the dinner and spoke in the subject of love, and the banquet becomes a party and a dinner. The voice continues saying*: someone else told me the story.* That person heard the story from Phoinix, the son of Philip who said that Apollodoros knew the story. The word Philip contains two syllables; (Phi) represents the prefix and is added in the beginning of (lip) to refer the mouth of man.

The son of Philip had nothing clear to say. Apollodoros must tell the story; he is the best man to report the speeches of his friends and was asked: *Were you at the party?* Apollodoros answered: *Don't you know that Agathon has been abroad for many years?* He changed the subject of the question and introduced a new subject. Apollodoros spent the last three years with Socrates; he was taking care every day to know; he used to run all over the places, anywhere and thought of himself as a great fellow, but was more miserable than anyone.

Apollodoros was asked to narrate the party or banquet. He and his friends were boys and Agathon won the prize; the winning is rooted in struggle to gain as a victory in a contest. Agathon and his chorus offered the sacrifice of thanksgiving dinner; the offering is made by being present attending with devotion. The word (thanks) is rooted in thought and gratitude; giving is rooted in have and hold and define bestow by a formal action.

Apollodoros was asked who told him the story and was *the same man who told the story to Phoinix* who is the son of *Philip* who is the father of Phoinix who is translated Phoenix to refer Phoenician. The little man never wore shoes; the wearing comes from clothing a person. Phoinix was at the party; he was a lover of Socrates. The road to town does well by listening *as we go.*

Apollodoros and his friend spoke about the banquet while they were walking together; he believes in being *pretty well word-perfect;* he also believes in speaking philosophy and pursuing Wisdom that involve the attitudes of a human being. Hearing other people speaking on the subject of philosophy makes Apollodoros delighted in a high degree of gratification. Others kind of talking among rich men and money makers annoys and disturb Apollodoros who feel pity at the fact of those men who do nothing and believe that they are doing something.

Apollodoros believes in being mad and crazy; he heard that Aristodemos met Socrates with evening shoes on and asked where he was going so smart. Socrates responded that he was going to dinner; he had refused going at the victory feast and accepted the invitation and is the reason of making himself pretty *to go pretty to a pretty man!* Apollodoros believes that Aristodemos wasn't invited to dinner and asked about his feeling of going uninvited to dinner.

Come with me, we will pervert the proverb a bit, Socrates said to Aristodemos, *'When gents give dinners, gents may just walk in'* the proverb is a brief popular epigram and a paradoxical saying that has been already perverted by Homer who draws Agamemnon as *a very perfect gentle knight* and Menelaos as a *weak warrior.* Agamenon gave a feast and a sacrifice; he brought in Menelaos to the feast uninvited in despite of Menelaos being a low man, and Agamenon being a high man.

Giving bestow in the feast by honoring the deity. The sacrifice is offered by surrendering to the Essence of our humanity for the power and giving common being up into the power of Wisdom. Menelaos is in a low state of conscience and gather with self in the feast to bring his low state high. Agamenon and Menelaos seem to be the same human being. The low and high states differ by their personalities. The perverted proverb literally denotes the analogy between the words. The metaphor is a figure of speech.

One *falls* behind and succumbs; the falling drop oneself into the low state, unaware and wounded by lacking the power. The suffering is rooted on the bondage and lack of knowledge. We ruin ourselves by the leanings and must get up from the downward direction to stand in *the way* and apprehend thoughts. Our best friend is waiting. Doors open. Events take place and time. The servant serves self and inner information is revealed.

Socrates told his friend who never wear shoes to go ahead inside Agathon's house; the door was open and something ridiculous happened: The servant from inside lead him toward the others who were sitting on their respective couches. Socrates came upon them as they were about to begin dinner.

My dear Aristodemos said Agathon; you are in time to join us at dinner. Take your place beside Eryximachos. The low state of consciousness goes alone with the state of being a macho man. Aristodemos never wear shoes and has no standing; he gave up common being and the Supreme Being took place to make him better with a higher state of conscience.

Aristodemos washed his feet and another boy came to repot speeches. Socrates went into the porch next door and there he is standing. Socrates had already raised his low level of conscience to a higher level and is standing on that place, alone and is his *way*.

Serve the Feast. Put the choices before you. No one should direct. We all are equal as human being. The Feast is a Deed for power and knowledge. We learn to defeat the ego. Ego commands rely on low level of conscience. The word Feast is rooted in the quality of invocating as a petition during a service of worshipping. Contemplating bring attention into the service. The devotion to the Spirit is a private worship in the state of being dedicated and loyal.

I never tried this before. *This* refers an aside dish in a foot note at the bottom of the page. *Imagine being invited to dinner* and *serve us to earn our compliments*. Agathon keep giving orders, and Socrates came in the middle of diner.

Aghaton reclines on the lowest seat. Foot note: *Lowest in dignity, at the end, on the right. It was taken in politeness by the host. They reclined in twos* (Low and high states of conscience. Agathon told Socrates: *I want to get hold of you to enjoy your wise thought*, and Socrates sat down. *What a blessing if Wisdom could run from the fuller to the emptier by touching one another like two cups placed side by side.*

A bit of wool would convey water from the fuller to the emptier! If Wisdom is like that, it is precious being side by side to be filled up with fine Wisdom. Wisdom means domination of wishes and desires; Wisdom empties us from the trash learned and fills us with valuable information about our humanity.

Agathon said to Socrates *you are a scoffer. We will come into court on our claim for wisdom and the judge shall be Dionysos.* Foot note: *Dionysos or Bacchus, god of wine, who loosens care and inspires to music and poetry.* Scoffer is rooted on mockery; the expression of scorn signifies contempt and defines the state of mind of one who despises. The word *wisdom* in small (w) defines scientific learning. Wisdom in capital (W) refers the ability to discern inner qualities and its relationship. The word Bacchus in the foot note is derived from Greek *Bakchos* and define the Greek god of wine called also Dionysus.

Now, first turn to dinner, said Aristodemos, and they all had their dinner pouring drops of grace and sang and chant to the god and settled down to drink. The short prayer at the meal asks for blessing and gives thanks. Pausanias began his speech by questioning *Look here, gentlemen how shall we manage our drinking most conveniently?* Aristodemos refers Pausanias'question and says that is a good advice to make drinking comfortable and that he himself had a good soaking the day before. The gentlemen at the dinner are all equal. Soaking intoxicate by drinking alcoholic beverages.

Eryximachos wanted to know how Agathon feels about being fit to drink, but Agathon doesn't feel fit; he was the strongest head for drinking, but had thrown up the sponge, and the rest are the *weaklings* of the mind. Drinking brings to the state of being drunk by excessive consumption of alcoholic beverages.

Socrates can do both ways: Being and no being and participate in common affairs without being drunk. The ego's commands had been stopped and there are choices; Socrates is not counted, and no one present votes for a hearty *bout of deep wine for drinking;* Socrates' moral responsibility is to help the others and isn't expected that anyone be offended by telling the truth about the effect of getting drunk.

From the physician viewpoint, drunkenness is dangerous to mankind and is the learned; the physician is un-willing to drink too much or advise others to do so, especially when having a headache from the drinking of previous day. There is an agreement of not to drink too much during the banquet; everyone should drink just to please the desire without going over the edge. The physician begins his speech by quoting the words of Euripides; he neither has a thought nor a theme; he noticed that many gods have hymns and *Paeans* made by poets and that *Love, the ancient mighty god has not one.*

Worthy professors compose praises to honor men like Heracles. A book lauded salt to the *skies* for its usefulness, and many other books can be found expressing favorable judgments. No a human being has ever dared to challenge Love, the great god that is neglected. There is plenty to entertain in the speeches, and a *full-dress Oration* praising Love is proposed by the physician. Each Oration begins from left to right. The Father of the speech begins first and is set in the first place. Foot note: *He sat furthest on the left, in the place of honor.*

Oration represents the Spanish speech and begins on the left and concludes in the right side. The verb represents the action and the main part of the Oration.

Socrates professes Love by practicing his affection; he has knowledge. His Love arises by his kindness and tenderness felt by the lover who is attached to enthusiasm and devotion; Socrates is loyal and benevolent who concerns for the good of others. *Aphrodite* in the Greek mythology refers the Greek *goddess of Love and Beauty;* the goddess lacks the god and the Beauty. Foot note: *Socrates and Agathon on the lowest couch on the right.* It is believed that *good speeches* does because people are always ready to believe what is heard, but hardly can they remember; many people have bad memory.

What is remembered is that love is a great god; he is wonderful on earth and in heaven; the god is honorable as being among the most ancient of all the others god. The people of Ancient Greece honored nine gods, but *Parents Love has none,* and they are no mentioned by anyone poet or not, and according Hesiod, Chaos comes first. Hesiod refers *Theogonia* in an account of the origin of the descendant of the gods. Love is *the ever lasting seat* of all of us. For many, *contrived love* is a devise or plan to handle situations; planning projects the achievement in the mind. The plan is constructed by the contriver who is a human being who manages the situation.

The greater good of mankind is the lover. The greater good of the lover is a beloved. The lover loves. The beloved loves self. The two are united and becomes One and the same. Love guides mankind through life, and without love, no man can accomplish beautiful works. Noble blood, ranks or wealth don't implant Love but shame at ugly things and ambition in beautiful things.

Man is often detected doing the ugly things; he allows himself to be treated in ugly fashion; his cowardice doesn't allow him to defend himself. On the other hand, a man who loves suffers less pain and is ashamed before the lover in an ugly situation. A *whole state or an army* can be made of lovers and beloved. They would abstain from all ugly things and from being ambitious. They would conquer Beauty by leaving the ranks and choosing to die many times. The immortality is Love and last forever.

The lover never desert the beloved, instead the lover helps in danger. Love inspires and influences Divinity; Love gives lovers power coming from self; on the other hand, *the gods breathes fury,* according Homer. The lovers gather in an affair to make love; the wife is willing to die for her husband, but surpasses love; they both are alien to each other and related only in name.

Alcestia was thought as noble possessing outstanding qualities of exalted rank and excellent properties. Her soul was sent up from the death in admiration for her deed. Noble deed count for those whom gods gives the privileges of having their soul sent up again from Hades in the underground to abide after dead.

The properties are own qualities belonging and especially peculiar to each human being. Our human properties include virtue; the soul is our essence causing our lives; the soul is embodied in human beings; the Deed is the action of every human being; it is the action that allows knowing every human being.

God regards respect to live up to fulfill a mental state in a high esteem. The body dies and goes the underground. For some, the body re-appears after death to the senses; the apparition disregards substantial existence. Being present hold into the possessions and keep under restrain to make accountable to the moral obligation. Bestow put in use the possession into action. The Self belong to oneself and is of same identity.

A zither-player plays the instrument but doesn't die for its love *like Alcestia* who was willing to die for her husband. Aquiles was honored and sent to the *Island of the Blest*. He was told by his mother that if he killed, he would die, if not, he would return home and live to be an old man, and he choose his lover.

The gods admire above measure and honor because set high value to their lovers who plays personalities. *Achiles* is the lover and *Patroclos* the beloved; they play two personalities in every human being. Their gods do great honor and value for love's sake and reward when the beloved feels affection for the lover who does for his beloved. The lover is more divine than the beloved since is inspired. The gods honor the personality of *a man more than a woman*.

Love is the oldest of all the gods and most precious and has more power. Love provides virtue and happiness to mankind in life and dead. The speech of Phaidros was related by Aristodemos to Apollodoros.

Pausanias doesn't believes that Phaidros' rules were properly laid down, and he refers over drinking to praise the desire for drinking; he believes that there is more than one love, and that we ought to praise Love and its source called god; the Oldest god is motherless and daughter of Heaven; the dwelling place is where the god abide. The other god is younger and daughter of a man and a woman and is called common love; he believes that the *action comes out in the doing, when it is done right, it is beautiful, and when is not right done, it is ugly.*

Common love works at random and is felt by inferior man who loves women and bodies rather than soul. *They choose the most foolish persons to get something done and care for nothing whether right or wrong* and act at random doing the opposite. That kind of love springs from the *goddess* (Female god) and have a share for female and male. The other love springs from Heaven and has a share for male only. Love has no violence, and those inspired by the Love feel affection and are driven by the pure and simple Love and fall in Love with their minds. Those are ready to be with themselves all their lives living together.

Those with the younger love (common love) are ready to be with it always for their lives and live together, but the foolishness deceives and laughs at them. There ought to have a law against loving that way, so the mental state might not be spent on what is uncertain regarding *vice and virtue* of body and soul.

The law of love should be made *compulsory* for those who challenge foolishness; they say that is *ugly* to gratify lovers, but they have their focus on common love and see tactlessness and injustice; on the other hand, the law of Love is done *decently and lawfully* and cannot *fairly* brings discredit.

The law of love is confusing, but in different state of mind, the law can be understood. When human beings ignore the intellectual faculties, they say that is right gratifying lovers and wish to convince others, but they are unable to argue on the subject and consider the gratification *ugly under barbarians.*

The Perfect Law has absolute power. The philosophy pursues Wisdom and search for understanding of the moral values and human principles which is the essence of our humanity dealing with fundamental concepts. The law of love is profitable to their rulers; its subject is not great in spirit or *makes strong friendship* in a union; the love is implanted. Perfect Law is found by the experience. The Love grows strong and brings the ruler to an end.

The ruler of mankind is the ego; the ego is part of self-low esteem and low state of conscience that makes human being to function in reality and acquire different personalities; the ego makes human being *ugly*; the ego produces desire. Man gratifies the desire for drinking alcohol; excessive alcohol leads man to the personality of alcoholism which is the evil condition of the alcoholic man who grasps *habits of the ruler* and *cowardice of the ruled*.

The ruled is the man himself; he lacks courage and moral strength, but is not easy to understand. *It is called better to love openly than secretly* and to love *the highest and nobles born*. The nobility is the quality of being noble in rank; the state of aristocracy identifies the best individuals as the privileged class; the power is vested in a minority consisting of those believed the best of a state; the body of upper class is made up of hereditary nobility who are believed to be superior.

Wondering feels curiosity and encourages being inspired with hope to stimulate the state of curiosity. Winning the struggle gain the victory and succeed the state by allowing the lover. Begging asks for mercy and compassion; the forbearance is subjected to one's power and is blessed by the act of divinity in favor on those beseeching and swearing solemn oaths. The lover has a grace. Perfect law allows doing without *discredit*. The doing is the Beauty of mankind. Man alone is pardoned for breaking the oath that he has sworn.

Challenging foolishness does in pursuit of anything but Wisdom. Wishing to accomplish reaps greatest disgrace to win *money and public office. Slavish service* is done *as no slave would do to get the power.* The best friend is *sleeping at the door* in a low state of conscience. The enemy upbraids and reproach *flattery* with *bad manners.*

The oath of love is the matrimony, but has no force. *A full license* is given *to* the lovers. The law says to love and feels affection for each other. On the other hand, fathers place tutors in the loved ones and forbid to converse with them while the tutor receives order to see. *A thing* is considered *very ugly. The fact is that the* case is very complex. *A base man* is one who hasn't learned. He has the five senses from birth. He is a common lover who loves bodies but the body fades. *He violates any number of vows and promises.*

The *law wishes to test.* The testing is *won by political power. It enjoys pursuing one and eschewing the other;* the law set tasks and test the tasks to see which class the lovers belong. In the beginning everything is tested; the *next* thing is *to be won by money and political power*; the suffering is derived from lack of endurance and ability to withstand hardship and adversity dealing with the stress.

The failure despise by looking down with contempt and aversion. Despising regards negligence and worthlessness. The achievement of affection *is never bred. One road is left* by the Perfect law and is for the beloved to gratify the lover. The beloved is a human being who ought to praise Love which is his Beauty in the pursuit of Virtue.

The custom is wishing to serve another human being. We assume that one man can make another man better. We plunge into slavery by serving another person who never is satisfied by our services. The other person lacks Love and compassion for self and lack the ability to value anything. We expect to be praised by our doing, but are unaware of the kind of service we provide. We must serve our Beauty in order to be praised. One is praised when Love is felt. Love makes us better human being and then, we live in two worlds knowing who we are and what to do in reality.

We desire. We assume being better. Assuming takes upon oneself for granted and seizes us. We pretend (to have) and (to be). Pretending gives false appearance of being who we are not. We adopt personalities and scientific leanings. We are living the time of science and technology in the United States of America and wish to be.

Philosophy concerns knowledge of our humanity and the learning of our possessions. Virtue conform right standing, and the quality of the power benefits us. We become capable of dealing with the desires that makes us slave and acquire real power coming from ourselves.

Wisdom is a concept meaning domination of desires. The prefix of the word Wisdom means wish. The word Wisdom in capital (W) refers the ability to discern inner qualities (our possessions) to make better judgments. When the desire is present, we adopt a wise attitude and a course of action to succeed. Solomon succeeds and became the best judge of his time.

Discerning detects and discriminates in order to have the knowledge in the mind; discerning allows observing and comprehending. A wise man serves himself and worships his possessions; the man is characterized by his Wisdom that is marked by deep understanding and keen discernment; the man exercises sound judgments. The prudence is the ability to govern and discipline oneself by reasoning; our possessions are our resources to be better human being.

The education is a process. Being educated is a stage and a state of mind and conscience; the educational process results in the development of knowledge. The field of study in the United States of America deals with methods of teaching and learning of science and technology in schools. The stage of being deals with the learning (to be), and we learn to play roles to earn the living.

The mind recollects memory, and we perceive. Perceiving attains understanding of objects. The word (under-stand) means being below capacity, and we ignore our system of intelligence and follow regulations of institutions. We have the intention to play roles, and we call playing (working) and are responsible to the role we play. We judge and have opinions based on a point of view. Focusing with intention of being leads to be good role player. Our state of conscience is low. The low state of conscience is the fact of being conscious of external objects concerning society and political cause. The low state of conscience is the normal state, and the mind is identified with unconscious process. A high state of consciousness leads to being aware of who we really are. We are human beings living unaware of our moral responsibilities and responding as role player.

The word con-science is rooted on being conscious of our moral goodness, conduct and intentions. We have the responsibility to be better human being. The conscience is a principle to enjoy. The word conscience lose its prefix (-cons), and only science is left. Science defines the kind of knowledge and differs from the knowledge of our humanity. The knowledge covers the truths and operates the Perfect Law called (natural science) Science are methods designed by man who has scientific knowledge. The prefix (-cons) translate (with) into the English language. A prefix is an affix. The affix is attached at the beginning of the word science. We are living the time of science and technology in the United States of America. The civilization relates the level of learning to function. Functioning ignore the intellect. The stage develops writing without using the meaning of words.

We put the words to function in the sentence. The words violate syntax of the English language and create plenty of room for interpreting. A solemn Feast has been interpreted as a banquet and a party. The word solemn indicates the kind of Feast marked by the invocation. Solemnity defines the condition or quality of being observing an event in a ceremony with self. Feast is rooted on holiness and pleasure in an event honoring a deity known as God. Holiness is the state or quality of being holy.

The holism is a theory and signifies analysis of facts in their relation to one another. The universe is seen in terms of interaction with living organism. Theory is rooted in Greek (Theo) and deals with beliefs. Pleasure is rooted on (pleasing; the state deals with sensual gratification of the senses. Interpreting deals with the known and we read at the level that we are prepared to read. We express the conception in the mind; interpreting conceive beliefs, and we judge every circumstance, but beliefs are no concepts and don't bring into realization.

The Perfect law meets together. The beloved gratifies the lover and never otherwise. The pursuit of riches gratifies a lover supposed to be rich, but is deceived and gets no money because the lover turns out to be poor. We show what lay in us. For money, we would do any service. If we gratify another as being good, we expect the other to be better because of the affection for he lover, but the other turns out to be bad and not possessed of virtue, and we are deceived, and the deceit is beautiful if the other means the ego; it shows what lay in it. In both cases, it is beautiful to gratify for the sake of virtue.

Love compels lover and beloved to take care of virtue; any other love is a common love and is Pausanias' contribution to the subject on praising Love, then, Pausanias paused upon the clause of how the *stylists teach him to jingle.* Aristodemos the reporter of speakers call Aristophanes to speak next, but *he had a hiccup* and couldn't speak; then, the reporter called Eryximachos who was reclining in the place below.

My dear Eryximachos, it's your job either to stop my hiccup, or to speak for me until I stop myself Eryximachos applies what had learned and advise to hold the breath for *a long time*; if the hiccup continues, gargling water should stop the hiccup; if the hiccup still goes strong, tickling the nose to sneeze is recommended.

Remember that Apollodoros heard the story of the banquet from Aristodemos. According Eryximachos *Pausanias began* his speech *well and ended feebly and deficient in qualities.* Eryximachos believes in putting a good ending to the oration representing Spanish speech. He says that *Love* is double. The art of medicine has a great god that extends over human and divine; the art is a skill acquired by experience; the divine defines the kind of god. The god is in the Souls of mankind and directs Beauty. He is also in the rest directing many other things.

The rest is a stoppage; it stands back and regards human needs. He is in the bodies of all living creature and *in what grows on earth and everything there is.* Eryximachos begins his speech about medicine; he already had honored his art by stopping the hiccup. The natural body has double love: Health and disease, and the two are common consent approving what is done. *There is one love in the healthy and another in the diseased.*

The healing art deals with gratifying health and temperance to be moderated as the bodies themselves gratify moderation, and the gratification must be done, and gratifying diseases must not be done.

The healing art deals with the knowledge of the body's love. The body is filled with good things and is emptied from the bad things, but should be empty first in order to be filled. A complete physician distinguishes the good from the bad love. A good practitioner makes changes and get one love where ought to be and takes out the love that is in, but should be taking out the kind of love in and get the Love we ought to have.

The ability is making friends from the greatest enemies who *are the most opposite.* Hot and cold, bitter and sweet, dry and wet are examples of the opposition. Our ancestors and fathers composed our art. They knew how to implant love and conquered it; the implanting inserts in a living creature and form an organic union. The conquering gain and master over. The healing art is guided by the correspondent god. There are many gods, one for each subject.

One at variance with itself is brought together again *like a harmony of bow and lyre*, but it is illogical saying that harmony is at variance with itself or that harmony is made up of notes still at variance. Eryximachos is at variance with his speech. The subject is praising Love, but he introduces several other subjects and causes the variance made of high and low. The harmony is a symphony and a kind of agreement. *Rhythm is made from quick and low; it* differ in the beginning and is brought into agreement.

Music plays agreement as the art of healing does. *It implants concord and love for each other*; music is the knowledge of love affairs concerning harmony and rhythm; it is not difficult to distinguish the love affair since the double love isn't there yet. The composer of rhythm and harmony is called *melody-making.* The use of the melodies and verses already made is called *education,* but there are difficulties and *a good craftsman is wanted.*

The decent man must be gratified, and the love must be protected. The love having *many hymns and polymnia* is the common love; the polyhymnia is the Greek Muse of sacred songs. The common love must be offered to people with great care. The love reaps pleasure and don't implant *temperance.* It is a great business like the art of healing. Hungry concerns the art of cookery, and people reaps the pleasure of eating. We must watch what we eat in order to protect ourselves as far as we can since there are many kind of love.

The compositions made by the melody-maker are full of common love. Love toward each other gets harmony and moderation and brings good health to mankind. Love brings vegetables and plants to other animals without harm. Violent love does harm and destroys, and pestilences come as the result. There are other discordant diseases in the *wild beast. Blights* come from the grasping of bad habits and indecency of such love affairs and business.

Sacrifice offers to a deity. The domain of divination is the common union between the gods and man together. Divination lacks the knowledge; it seeks and foretells. The mind perceives *impiety;* it is the quality of lacking respect; impiety is to occur *if one does not gratify decent Love and honor him and put him first in every work;* impiety is what divination is ordered to do, *to supervise, and* (vise) of super-vise hold the force and *treat them as a physician.*

Divination is the craftsman of friendship between man and god. Its knowledge about mankind tends towards good law and piety and inspire. The Love has great power; its Omnipotence is the state of unlimited power. It concerns with accomplishing with moderation and justice. It provides happiness and makes us able to help others.

The Love is higher than we are. We are in a lower state of conscience. The next speech correspond Aristophanes. His hiccup is gone *but not until sneezing was applied which made him wonder in the decency of the body desiring noises and tickling to sneeze.* Aristophanes is playing the fool when is about to make his speech. He laughed. He doesn't wants to be watched anymore. He doesn't feel fear. He promises that his speech would be clear and natural to his god. He intends to speak in a different way. He believes that mankind failed to perceive the power of Love and built the greatest sanctuary and ought to be done.

Love helps mankind. Love is the healer of those healing and the greatest happiness to the human race. Aristophanes announced the introduction of the power to teach others. The nature of man and its history must be learned. The natural state isn't the present state. There are two personalities male and female. The present state is translated from Latin *Status quo. The shape of mankind was round. The status Quo Antes* corresponds before the birth. Ribs passes from back to front in a circular shape and corresponds the body.

Two personalities imagine four arms with equal amount of hands to manipulate. Two faces on a round neck are exactly alike. There is one head with two opposite faces and four ears. Two *privy* members relate his individuality and *rest* to be free from walking in any direction he wants. The man run fast by rolling over and over on the end of the eight limbs; it assigns limitation and restrictions. The male is said born of the sun; the female is said born from the earth. Both male and female have something from the moon and refers dependency. Both the earth and the moon depend from the sun for light and heat, and human being have the force of ambition.

Ambition has an ardent desire for rank, fame and power. Rank relates the standing or position of playing roles. Fame is rooted on speaking and public estimation like reputation and popular acclaim. Power is rooted on capacity and ability to manage or control own desires. *There were three sexes. The third one has both sexes together and was called Hermaphrodite. The beast have four arms, two faces, on a round neck looking alike; The beast have one head with two opposite faces and four ears. The beast has two privy members and walked in any direction he wants,* but cannot be allow going in the wild way.

Aristophanes believes that man can be stopped from violence by making him weaker. Each man can be sliced through the middle. The slicing in two half could make mankind more useful. Man should walk upright on two legs; if he chooses to continue wild, he deserves to be sliced again, so he *hop on one leg like those on the wineskins at the fair.* The slicing can be done *as you slice your serviceberries through the middle for pickle or as you slice hard-boiled eggs with a hair.* The face could be turned half the neck toward the cut to make man see own cut and be more orderly and heal the rest up. Turning the face gather the skin over the belly.

The purses pull and shut with a string. A little mouth is made to fasten it at the middle of the belly in the navel. The wrinkles at the belly are smoothed. The breast is shaped. The original body is cut to allow each half wanted the other and hugged it. Each half throw their arms around each other desiring growing together in the embrace, but they died from starvation and general diseases as they weren't willing to do anything apart from each other. *When one of the halves died and the other is left, it hunts for another half of a whole woman or man.*

Hermaphrodite is a translation from Greek and is attributed to homosexuality. The prefix *–homo* in Latin refers mankind and is rooted in *homoman*. *Hermaphroditos* in the Greek epic refers the son of Herman and *Aphrodite*. *Aphrodite* was the Greek goddess of love and beauty. The information is about our body, and we ought reasoning.

The hormones are living cells that circulate in body fluids and produce specific effect in our behavior. *Beast* lack reasoning. A beast epic converts the wild behavior.

The epic narrate our deed. *The Iliad and the Odyssey* is examples of epic. The education allows learning about our humanity. We acquire the knowledge in a Feast with ourselves and learn of the existence of a Lord called God who teaches us about ourselves. We respect and attend in Spirit and are influenced by rendering the tribute. God stands for Generation, Order and Delivery.

The weakness of mankind is rooted on lacking power. Mankind lacks ability to reason and is deficient. The weakness allows functioning without reasoning and performing as a robot. We learn skill and become skillful. We ought to move alone as a better human being. We must choose better ways of living. The alternative helps us to accomplish what we ought to be. We deserve being worthy rather than fitting in our society. We deserve being rewarded for what we really are.

Serving perform to receive the benefit of worshipping our human principles and turning ourselves to the state of being better human being. We have the capacity of provoking changes in ourselves. We acquire abilities to see own human condition needing to be healed and restored to purity. The energy for healing is sleeping and keeps us in a low state of conscience. We must be aware of our human condition of being and also of our human principles for being better. Our low state of conscience is characterized by our functioning without considering our intellectual faculties.

Another different scheme was found to educate mankind. The privy parts are moved to the front to make generation come between male and female and the human race continues. The gathering of two men satisfies their union. They *turn to work and care general business of life. Mutual love is ancient. The love is implanted in mankind.* The love brings the *parts together trying to make one out of two and heal the nature structure of man.*

Aristophanes believes that each of us is the tally of a man who was *sliced like a flat fish, and the two half made one man.* Each half seeks its other tally. The man who is cut from the old common sex called *manwoman* is fond of women and *adulteresses.* Women who are cut of the ancient women don't care of man. The women who are cut from male pursue the male and are fond of men. *Those women enjoy lying with men and embracing them and are the best.*

The men are brave and are called shameless. The common love grows up on public affairs and is fancy. They don't *trouble about marriage.* The lover welcomes *what is akin;* those engaged in the affair cannot say what is expected from the other. On the other hand, no one suppose that is a sensual union conveying the kind of relationship. The senses are our faculty of perceiving the natural mechanism of sight, hearing, smelling, tasting and touching. The sensory of those mechanisms constitute a distinct unit that differs from other mechanism as is a thought.

The union of a common human being with its Supreme Being allows loving self and makes anyone delighted. Boldness is being fearless before danger assuring confidence and courage. Our Soul wants the other Love. The Soul discovers intuition.

The Soul riddles to find solutions of our common problems. The Soul lies together with us standing besides us as a tool for us to question on what we want. Commonly, we please our desires; the desire is present for us to manage and learn from its sensing. We don't want to be melted and welded together with common love and make one of two. That kind of love doesn't last long.

We want Love. It last forever after we die. The passion is to think rather than assume; passion is a state of being full of strength; passion is characterized by the action. Believing heard what is desired. We don't believe in being united together with the beloved and become one of two. The unity is our ancient natural shape. The desire for the whole and the pursuit of it is *named Love.*

Common love is full of fear; we are not decent; *we may be sliced in half again and go like many relief carvings of persons shown in half view on tombstones, sawn right through the nose, like tally-dice cut in half.* We must exhort *to be good learning man* to escape the fate and attain our desires. Love is our leader *and captain* and let no man oppose it. When we are reconciled with the God, we enjoy own beloved.

Aristophanes commands and doesn't want that Eryximachos makes fun of his speech. He doesn't want being interpreted as Pausanias and Agathom. He believes that he has spoken in general about human beings. He believes that *the way of making human race happy is to make love perfect.*

We ought to get own beloved by going back to our original nature; it is a beloved who suits our minds and automatically, we praise Love who is always present giving and blessing and bringing us home where we belong. The beloved offers the greatest hope. We worship our human principles and we will be restored to our ancient nature healed, blessed, and happy. Aristophanes believes that his speech is very different from the speech of Eryximachos.

Agathon begins his speech and wishes to describe how he ought to speak, and then, begin speaking. Agathon believes that mankind has been congratulated in the speeches spoken and that the god that causes changes in mankind has no been spoken. The god that causes changes gives the gifts, but has not been described. The *laudation* is first, to describe who god is and what it causes, and then, praise the god for what it is and praise its gifts.

According Agathon, all gods are happy. Love is the happiest of all the gods. Love is Beauty and *the youngest of the gods he flies in full flight away from Old age;*

Common love *hates old age* and don't come near it. The love is always associated with the young *and with them, he consorts.* The old business is done through *Necessity.* The truth tells of Love and friendship and peace. Love reign over the gods. Love is young and tender. A poet like Homer is needed to show the god's tenderness. He says about presumptuous madness *at least her feet were tender.*

> He says: *Tender are her feet*
> *She comes not near the ground,*
> *But walks upon the head of men.*

Agathon believes that good proof of tenderness is given. The walking is not in the hard, but on the soft. Love walk not on the earth, nor on top of heads. Love walks and abides in the softest things. His abode is settled in the tempers and Souls of gods and men. Love departs with hard temper. *Since he always touches the softest of the soft,* Love must be tender.

If Love were stiff, it could not fold himself throughout every soul and comes and go unnoticed. *His gracefulness is a great proof of his proportion and supple shape.* Love has in high degree. There is always war between gracelessness and Love. Colors and beauty testifies its god. Love sits in the fragrance of the flowers and there, it stays.

Chief is that Love wrongs not and is not wronged, wrongs no god and is wronged by none, wrongs no man and is wronged by none. Violence touches not Love. Love serves Love in everything. Love is full of temperance. It is the master and control of pleasures and desires. No pleasure is stronger than Love. Courage doesn't stand against Love. It is not the god of war who hold Love, but love war. Stronger is he who holds rather than being held. The master of the bravest is himself being the bravest. One must try to do the best. One is able to do so. Love is so wise a poet, that he can make another the same. Everyone to whom Love touches becomes a poet including those who can't have music in their souls. Love is good poet and the creation of fine arts.

No one cannot give what don't have or teach others what don't know. The maker of all living things disputes the clever work of Love. Art turns out notable and illustrious. Where there isn't touch of Love, it is all in the dark. Archery, medicine and divination were invented and led by desire and love. The business of the gods was arranged; love of beauty is plain. There is no Love in ugliness. Many terrible things happened to the gods because of the reign of *Necessity*. The common love is born for men loving beautiful things. Love comes first and causes beautiful things to others. *It is he who makes Peace among men, calm weather on the deep, Respite from winds, in trouble rest and sleep.*

He empties us of strangers and fills us with friendliness. It ordains the present meeting of people one with another in the feast, in sacrifices and becomes men's guide. It provides gentleness and vanish savagery; Love loves giving good will. Love illustrates the wise and admires the gods and treasures those who have some of him. The god cares of good things and careless of bad things. Love saves, and man must follow. Love charms the mind. When Agathon had spoken, all the rest applauded. Agathon's speech was the best of his abilities.

Socrates begins his speech. He believes that Agathon was quite right in the beginning of his speech when he announced that he would first show what Love was, and afterwards define its works. Socrates admires the beginning of the speech describing what Love is. He wanted to know whether the love described by Agathon is the love for objects or not. Socrates makes clear that he doesn't refer the love of mother or father, but the love that can be applies to *Father*.

Socrates wanted to know whether the father is the father of something, like father of son or daughter and whether a brother is the brother of something or the brother of sister, and he question: *Is Love love of nothing or love of something?* Socrates wants the object of love to be remembered and whether the love desires the object. Socrates asked what happens when love has what is desired. He would consider the word necessity and applies the word in a question *isn't it necessary that desiring desires what it lacks?* He believes that is absolutely necessary.

No one being big wants to be big, and no one being strong wants to be strong. The reason is that no one lacks what he already has. Human beings have power whether whished or not. Human beings are possessed of riches and health and strength and wish to go on being possessed of them in the future. Mankind has the possession at present whether wanted or not. Love bless being preserved into the future and being always present.

Any one, who desires, desires what is not in his possession; it is himself; the existing love is an object. The assumption arranges their business through love of objects. Usually, human beings want what don't have, and the love for objects is full of fear and lacks knowledge.

The speeches about love are fine, but the truth about our humanity cannot be contradicted. Socrates heard a speech about love affairs from his female teacher. He narrates the speech by first describing what love is and its works. He believes that love is a great god and a love of beautiful things, but is neither beautiful nor good and what is not beautiful is not necessary ugly. What is not wise isn't necessary ignorant. There is something between wishing and ignoring called perception.

Perceiving is having the right opinion without reasoning and is admitted by those who don't know about lover and beloved *you for one and I for another.* The called happy are those possessed of objects called good things. The love is admired by those who don't have the good things. They desire those things. The love is between mortal and immortal. The power is interpreted to ferry across the good things given by man.

The art of divination moves god's commands and *requitals* and returns and binds all together into a whole. The art of divination deals with priests and incantations. The art of divination is the source of witchcraft. God doesn't mingle with mankind. The communion, the conversations of gods with men and men with god comes from man. The one expert on those things is called spiritual man. The expert in the common arts is a vulgar man. A feast was held when Aphrodite was born. The party was held by the gods among Plenty. After they had dined, *Poverty came in begging. Plenty* got drunk and went to the park and fell asleep. *Poverty* planed to have a child from *Plenty* and lay by his side and conceived from making love. The love becomes follower and servant of Aphrodite. The son of *Plenty* and *Poverty* gets their fortunes, but he is always poor and far from being tender.

He is unshod and homeless lying on the ground without bed sleeping by the doors in the streets in the open air. He had inherited his mother's nature and dwell with wants. From his father he had inherited being brave, a mild hunter of the truth. He elaborates the possessions. He is a successful coveter of wisdom and desires what belong to another. He lacks knowledge. He is a great wizard and influences others.

The son of *Plenty* and *Poverty* was born neither mortal nor immortal, he is blooming and alive in the same day when has *Plenty*. Sometimes, he is dying and gets life through his father's nature. *What he procures in Plenty always trickles away.* Love is neither in wanting nor in wealth but between desiring and ignoring. No god wishes to become wise. The worse of ignorance is one who is neither beautiful nor intelligent and think of himself being good enough to desire the high qualifications. He doesn't think that he is lacking thinking in what he needs and is reasoning over assuming.

The so called philosophers are between wishing and being wise. Wishing is a common thing. Loving is a love for beautiful things. The birth of the love is rooted in being wise and is the nature of mankind. Anyone wishing to have good things gets happiness. The wishing itself is the feeling of happiness and don't need to ask for happiness because is already present.

The Diagram

- Focusing lack order and deceive the constructor of the diagram.

- The personal names in the diagram represent personalities, but the role played is not who they are.

- Being is contradicted, and no-knowing is complemented.

- The judgment lacks subject.

- Diner is a man who dines; he reclines towards his left; he uses his right hand to help himself, and a large cushion is used under his left arm.

- There isn't silverware to eat dinner.

- The state of being of the wine in the note explaining the diagram is usually drunk and mixed with three parts of water.

- Cena translates dinner into the English language.

- Dinner is the last meal of the day in the United States of America.

- Supper is the last meal of the day in Spain and Dominican Republic.

The word diagram is rooted on marking by lines; the word was used in (1619) to explain graphic design; a diagram shows arrangement in relationship with its parts, and each part explains rather than represent.

The diagram is constructed of hyphens in a circular shape and has thirteen smaller circles; there are two hyphens between the circles around it.

Seven of the small circles are drawn with bolt point; four of the bolt pointed circles are assigned names and identity, and the remaining three are assigned name only. A line separates the name from the identity; the names belong above the line; the identity belongs below the line.

Phaidros is underlined *("Father of the speech")*; the identity is enclosed within parenthesis; double quotation marks within the parenthesis indicate that the words were borrowed for the construction of the diagram.

Aristophanes is underlined (*The comic poet; had hiccup*); the identity is enclosed within parenthesis; Aristo is added at the beginning of the name. The prefix was used in Britain (1864) to refer aristocrat and member of so called (Noble); they believe in being superior; prefix is an affix added in the beginning of words, and affix is an attachment. *Comic* defines the kind of poet, and hiccup is defined as a spasmodic inhalation with closure of the glottis accompanied by a peculiar sound; Aristophanes miss-represent the poet.

Eryximachos is underlined (*Physician*); the identity is enclosed within parenthesis (-Machos) represent machismo; the suffix is attached at the end of the name. Eryximachos plays the role of physician

Aristodemos is underlined (*Who reported the speeches*) the identity is enclosed within parenthesis; the suffix is attached at the end of the name; (-demos) is rooted on Demagogue (1831) and signify populace; they were the common people of Ancient Greek state; Aristodemos plays the role of reporter. The name is made up of two attachments.

Six of the bolt pointed circles are assigned numbers. Number (l) is followed by number (2) and is followed by number (4); numbers continues backward with number (3) and upward with number (5) followed by number (6) Phaidros is assigned Number (1). Number (2) is assigned to (Pausanias); number (4) is assigned to Eriximachos; number (5) is assigned to Agathon, and number (6) is assigned to Socrates.

The other six small circles are drawn of smaller hyphens; two of the six hyphened circles are labeled (Not reported); two of the remaining four are labeled (Left early); one of the remaining two is assigned name and labeling, and the last one no-name or labeling is assigned, and only one of the circles is assigned number (7) correspondent to Alcibiades who is underlined (The Statesman came in late, drunk) The identity is enclosed within parenthesis; Alcibiades plays the role of statesman.

An arrow inside the diagram is made of dashes and is labeled *from left round to the right.* Another smaller arrow inside the diagram contradicts the first arrow and begins on the right side of the circle and extends toward the left side continuing downward.

A note explaining the diagram appears under the drawing; an argument is introduced and constructed with third person singular and present indicative of be.

The diagram represent the subject of the statement, and the auxiliary of (be) represents state of being of the diagram; the word *drawn* after the auxiliary of (be) complements the subject and is called subject complement.

A contradiction is introduced and constructed with adverb (not) after (is) the adverb contradict state of being; pronoun (it) function subject of the contradiction, and adverb clause beginning with (how) complements not knowing the arrangement of the couches.

An assumption is introduced and constructed with past tense form of the verb;

The couches represent the subject of the sentence; *two person each* is functioning direct object of the verb and *some were made longer* functions subject complement.

A prepositional phrase beginning with (from) introduce an opinion constructed with the present tense form of the verb; neuter pronoun (It) is functioning subject of the judgment; (seems) represent the act of the subject; (that) introduces a noun clause;

Each diner represents the subject of the clause; *reclined* represents the verb of the clause; *toward his left* functions direct object of verb; *supported under his left arm by a large cushion and his right hand free to help himself from a low stool or table in front of the couch)* functions subject complements.

An expression is introduced and constructed with auxiliary (have); plural pronoun (They) function subject of the expression; auxiliary (Had) miss-represent the act of the subject and function adjective, and *no knives or forks* define the predicate; the coordinating conjunction allows option between silverware.

A statement of belief is introduced and constructed with the third person singular and past tense form of (be); *the wine* represents the subject of the statement; the auxiliary of (be) represents the state of being of the wine and define the predicate; *usually drunk mixed with water* and *three parts of water to two of wine* is functioning subject complement

The word *vases* are used to construct a prepositional phrase and indicate the plural form of the noun; vase holds wine and is derived from (vas); ancient vice define corruption of mankind and is replaced by *ancient vases.*

Diner defines a man who dines and gives dinner to others; he reclines towards his left and is supported by a large cushion under his left arm; his right hand is free to help himself from a low stool or table placed in front of the couch; there is an option between furniture signifying one or the other; *table* is used to place dishes with dinner; a *low stool* is placed in front of recliner to rest the feet after dinner; *couches* is the plural form of couch; the seat for two people is placed at the table to sit down and eat dinner; the word couch was used in the 14th century.

The word diner was used in (1815); dinner is the principal meal of the day in the United States of America; the food is prepared at dinner time around (5PM); there is an option between silverware signifying one of the other; the silverware is used to eat dinner at the table; knife is used to cut, and fork hold the food.

Wine is rooted on (win) (before 12th century); wine is currently used in the service of Christian communion; the fermented juice of fresh grapes is a beverage that might intoxicate dependent on the amount of wine drank; *two parts of wine* are mixed with *three parts of water*; the whole wine contain five parts $(2/5 + 3/5 = 5/5 = l)$

Drunk is being intoxicated with wine; a drunkard is usually drunk and a name calling; drank is the past participle form of drink.

Giving wine correspond the transitive verb form. Wined and dined represent the past tense form of the verbs. Wineglass is a glass for drinking wine. Winegrower is called to a person who cultivate vineyard; the noun was used on (1844). Wine press is a machine that extracts the juice from grapes to make wine. Winery was called the business of making wine. Wine shop is called a tavern specialized in serving wine. Wineskin is a bag made from the skin of some animals for holding bottles of wine.

The Banquet at Agathon's House, 416 B.C and *Diagram showing order of reported speeches* appears under the diagram; (B.C) are the initials of Before Christ; the word banquet is rooted on bench and bank (15th century) and is defined as an elaborated and often ceremonious meal for numerous people in honor of a person; banquet is translated into the English language from Latin (Feast); banquet room in hotels and restaurants is suitable for banquets; banquette is called to a long upholstered bench.

Cena translate dinner into the English language; the last meal of the day is called supper in the Spanish culture and is served in the evening time; the appointed time of meal is the time of eating the meal. The room where Christ and his disciples had supper is called Cenacle; the word is rooted on Latin Cenaculum and is used to signify the last meal of the day

The word (Cena) can be found on page 393 of <u>The Greek and Roman Antiquities Dictionary</u> by W. Smith W. Wayte, and G.E Marinden, 3rd edition; the word *Symposium* can be found on page 741 of same dictionary; Symposium is a Latin word for a social gathering; the formal meeting purpose the interchange of ideas between several specialists who deliver speech on a topic or related topic.

Symposion was used in (1603) in Ancient Greece for drinking together in a banquet; the party included music, and conversation. A Symposiarch was called to a person who presides over a symposium. A symposiast was called to a person who contributes to a symposion (1656);

The intention of constructing a diagram concluded in the construction of the diagram; the constructor determinates to construct, and the determination is the process of constructing; the diagram becomes the product of the intention directed to the object called diagram; the intention purposed to construct and is accomplished; intention implies what is in the mind, and *the diagram is drawn circular for convenience.*

Maria L. Marquez.